MEMORY AND HOW WE ~~LOSE~~ USE IT

VANESSA MILES

ALSO BY THE AUTHOR

A Capital Guide For Kids

Castles and Dungeons

What Can I Do?

Family Guide to London

For Arlo and Gracie

PART ONE

MEMORIES ARE MADE OF THIS

PART TWO

CARE AND MAINTENANCE

INTRODUCTION

Everything we do is affected by our memory. Our personal world is shaped by it, our sense of existence relies on it, allowing us to dip into our past, hang on to the present and imagine the future. It comes into sharp focus when we need it and retreats silently into our subconscious when we don't.

In the grand scheme of things, it's only comparatively recently that the intricacies of memory have been studied and even less time since any conclusions have been reached. But thanks to advances in brain imaging techniques, scientists have made giant strides in their understanding of how memory functions. New discoveries emerge on a daily basis forcing us to redefine our perceptions of what goes on inside our head.

It's all too easy for us to forget what an exceptional mechanism we have at our disposal. Although it can sometimes be unpredictable and we might find ourselves asking the question: "whose side are you on?" we realise it's on our side working for us, even during those moments when it appears to be taking an alarmingly long lunch break.

By examining how it lets us down, the tricks it plays on us, its ability to falsify even simple events, its knack of recalling the most unlikely and trivial things as well as our basic and vital need to forget, this book will set the reader on an exploration through the highways and byways of this incredible device we call memory.

There has been much talk of the benefits of brain training and exercise. Doing a crossword, tackling Sudoku puzzles or magazine quizzes that make the mind run twenty laps are believed to make a big difference. In the same way as going to a gym and working out makes us feel healthier and fitter, so too with memory.

The idea behind writing this book, however, is to provide a much broader brief. There are exercises to stimulate the brain and facts that are quite literally mind boggling. But above all we see how truly remarkable our memory is and how it plays a central role in defining the course of each activity we do and every thought we have.

The book, rather like the brain itself, is full of 'synaptic connectors' linking the unusual, amusing, amazing and sometimes even the downright bizarre.

It's no accident that the first and most important piece of engineering for a modern computer, one that uses the language of the brain to describe it, is RAM, or to give it it's proper title, Random Access Memory. The brain got there first.

PART ONE
MEMORIES ARE MADE OF THIS

1. TYPES OF MEMORY

"I remember my first joke. We were all having supper and Grandma asked if we'd like any more custard, and I passed my mat up instead of my plate and to my delight Grandma poured the custard over the mat. I was delighted that my joke had worked - but then I learnt something about comedy: everybody turned on me and said what did I do that for? They didn't ask Grandma why she poured the custard over the mat."

– Terry Jones

From the latest research, it's now reckoned that we function more like the goldfish than we imagined. Our lives, it's believed, are dominated by a three second window of experience. Apparently, we hug one another for three seconds, wave for the same amount of time and chew our food in a similar time-frame. It's universal, too. Whatever our gender or nationality we all follow the same pattern. And when it comes to remembering, we can only recognise and grasp the present in speedy three second bursts which are then linked together to allow us a continuous experience of the familiar world around us.

Of course, at the end of each three seconds everything becomes either the past and accessible through memory - or the future and so out of reach until it arrives. Oddly, if this three second period were to be increased to say, thirty seconds, we would start to encounter problems. For instance, it would be difficult to react to danger or to respond to other abrupt changes that might affect us unfavourably. We would dwell unduly on inessential details.

It's a strange thought but ultimately the greater part of our lives is experienced only via memory. It's our autobiography. It would be difficult to imagine a future event without using some experience from the past as a reference. What we think of as our immediate thoughts, feelings and actions that seemingly exist in the present, are in fact fleeting moments which must dissolve after a few seconds and quickly transform themselves into past events. The familiar disappears and is gone, becoming yet another new set of past experiences which we can reach once again solely through memory.

The way in which male and female brains are wired also affects how memory works. In women for example, the connections move from side to side making verbal and emotional clues such as events, dates etc. have a greater impact on memory than images - although women recognise faces, particularly female faces, more easily than men. For men, the connections on one side of the brain between the back and front account for better spatial and visual skills and thereby play a greater role in how men access memories.

These differences are also likely to be the effects of oestrogen versus testosterone as much as brain function. Research shows that when it comes to improving short-term memory, which includes formulating and storing memories, testosterone has the edge, but for long-term memory oestrogen is better.

Creating a memory involves...

encoding > storing > retaining > recalling

Accessing Data

Remember when encyclopedias were our search engines? Suppose we wanted to find out exactly when a certain State joined the United States and we have a stack of encyclopedias piled high in readiness. We might start our search at U for USA or S for States or perhaps A for American (sub section P for Political Union.) The list could turn out to be long and the books quite heavy.

Then imagine we change our mind about what we want to know. We must start all over again with another search in another book.

We need to improve things. We know what we want to find and our memory can remind us where to find it. But the books are still cumbersome and heavy.

Crucially, we must now add our imagination - our, 'what if ' moment. What if we had a computer that could store all that encyclopedic data for us? The link between the memory of tedious searches in books and how we might improve the process is key.

Of course, after we've stored all the data in our computer we might continue by designing an astute, 'finder' tool which can search for any subject we want. Suddenly all the monotonous page turning is gone. We can even invent a computer code to allow for human error - say a spelling mistake or perhaps we may not have given the computer enough information to carry out its serach - sorry, search!

Modern day computers are clever at accessing data and can provide extremely sophisticated criteria that refines that access. However, we alone choose and define how we wish the computer to act and what information is stored that is based on human memory and our creative vision of what it would take to make life better.

Just Like a Computer?

It may be tempting to compare human memory to the workings of a computer. Computing certainly borrows many of its terms from this most intricate and complex triumph of brain function and memory is, without doubt, the most advanced electrical system ever imagined. But it also operates with great subtlety.

Naturally, computers can also be programmed to do various forms of reasoning which is shown in things like the response of Google to the inputs we give it.

Nevertheless, the main task of a computer is to store, search and retrieve data and amazing though that might be, it's frankly undemanding. The human brain has a significant edge. It can gather data, but in addition it adds substantial extra elements like reason, emotion and imagination. And, of course, the brain also designs computers.

But imagine for a moment you decided to look up the details of a trip you made to Greece a couple of years ago. Just like Google, you'll instantly recognise the data but much of it will be irrelevant to you. You'll want to remember the holiday but not necessarily the flight number of the plane that took you there.

Whilst taking certain information on board, we also edit out substantial amounts of it. For example, if we type Greece into Google, results for our search might produce over six million results. If we think for a moment about the vast amount of information that can be stored via a computer we soon realise there is no possibility for us to remember it all, but then, nor would we want to.The need to remember is governed by feelings as well as fact finding.

A pivotal area of our brain, the Hippocampus, is our memory hub which among other things provides vital routes through which short-term experiences are solidified into long term memories. There's no doubt that the job of the neuroscientist would be far easier if there were more specific areas in the brain earmarked 'Memory' which constantly catalogued information, filing it away neatly or later use. To make matters worse, memories of specific subjects aren't neatly bundled together in a fixed area but are located in different regions of the brain. Although memories might be linked by association they are not necessarily retrieved from the same place. When we retrieve a memory, all the minute differences in the building blocks we use are personal to us and ultimately make us the individuals we are.

If we randomly took several facts about our first car, the smell of the interior, the seats or dials for example. Each person will recall specific separate memories from which they finally construct an overall picture.

It's quite possible too, that given the random nature of memory, the brain is careful not to put too many eggs in one basket and places items in different areas for good reason.

So...

Memory falls into two basic categories each with their own particular functions.

Long -Term Memory

Long-term memories, some of which stay with us forever, are a much more permanent fixture of our memory world. In order to hold on to them they must be encoded before storage is possible. Unlike a diary where everything is carefully filed away in one place, our long-term memories use a raft of connections to keep them in our mind's eye.

Long-term Memory is sub-divided into two main parts:

Explicit Memory

This is the conscious recall of events from our past. A holiday we took last Christmas, a specific trip to the cinema, our last birthday.

Implicit Memory

This is when we ride a bike for instance or drive a car - it's the instinctive kind of memory we use unconsciously.

Explicit Memory then has two main **subdivisions Semantic Memory and Episodic Memory**

Semantic Memory

involves knowledge aquired over the years - names, facts, recognising people

Episodic Memory

deals with personal experiences and specific long-term events - passing an exam, a first date dinner

Short-Term Memory

Short-term memory as the name suggests stays with us for a brief time only. It might be possible to remember a new telephone number or an address over a period of, say thirty seconds but it only stays with us for longer if we actively repeat the information we wish to hang on to, thereby storing it more permanently.

Even though short term memory storage ability is limited, it plays a vital part in our everyday life allowing us to put our thoughts and actions in order and to do several tasks at once. We use it for all manner of things from retaining long numbers - although seven seems to be the limit - to the name of someone we've just met, or where we left the magazine we were reading a few seconds ago.

Memory Recall - *stored in memory*
Q. What colour is the sky?
A. Blue.

Memory Recognition - *stored in memory but needs cues*
Q. What colour is the sky?
   Is it (a) Red (b) Blue or (c)Yellow?
A. Blue

This requires you to recognize the one answer which is correct. (see multiple-choice quiz page 128)

Memory Recognition can also involve accessing various random pieces of information which, once stored in our memory, can be retrieved easily but without any cue or prompt.

For example:
Q. Write down some facts about the sky.
A. The sky is big and blue but sometimes cloudy and grey.

The difference between Recall and Recognition can play a vital part in eye witness
testimonies. (see Recall and Recognition Test page 132)

Spool back... Can you remember the area of the brain where short- term experiences are solidified into long term memories?

2. THE ASTONISHING DIVERSITY OF MEMORY

"The difference between false memories and true ones is the same as for jewels: it is always the false ones that look the most brilliant."

— Salvador Dali

Childhood and Beyond

How far back can a memory be relied on? The painter Salvador Dali claimed to remember being in his mother's womb. A bit far fetched you might think and merely a figment of an extremely fertile imagination but his memory caught the eye of the press and public, a very useful situation for someone in the self-promotion game. Our own first memories are unlikely to go back that far but it's surprising how much comes to mind when we start to think about our childhood.

According to research, for most of us, significant and lasting memories begin when we are a little over three years old. Anything earlier is likely to be pieced together, simple fragments that we recall later as a solid memory tending more toward fiction than reality.

However, a friend's earliest memory is both vivid and convincing. It involves being in his pram as a baby. According to him it was dark blue with two fixing points on the right and left for attaching safety reins which were common at the time. He recalls the padded plastic edge of the prime side which was pale cream. This chewable surface became the perfect teething ring material and he remembers, over time, biting holes through it.

When we recall episodes from childhood we get a renewed sense of self. It helps define us and puts our particular stamp on what took place. However, in the process of remembering it is also probable we embellish events and fine tune the details to project a better personal picture, not only for anyone we may tell the story to, but for ourselves as well.

In his autobiography, the writer Mark Twain noticed that when he was younger he could remember anything, whether it had happened or not. But as he got older and his faculties diminished, he felt he would then remember only the things that never happened.

Occasionally, when someone's account of a moment varies from our own, the discrepancies can be so unexpected we are left open mouthed, wondering whether we witnessed the same event at all. This might not have anything to do with our failure to recall events accurately but more a question of a different perception of what took place at the time. An alternative perspective which can make us question our own reliability in recalling events in other areas.

The Comfort of Memory

Memory is personal. A subtle instrument we may use in order to invent a version of ourselves rather than a way of simply recalling information. It is also tempered by today's events and so is changeable, fragmented and ultimately illusive.

But how much do memories mislead or support us? In a negative and unfriendly world, the well-trodden routes which reinforce moments of certainty are reassuring. Times gone by appear better, summers hotter and childhoods safer. Our mind becomes a convenient refuge for particular episodes in the past which we return to often, making them more vivid than the actual event.

In fiction, memory has been described as connected to love and the more we love a memory the stronger and stranger it can become.

A character in Julian Barnes's novel, The Sense of an Ending, remarks that, "The longer life goes on, the fewer are those around to challenge our account, to remind us that our life is not our life, merely the story we have told about our life. Told to others, but – mainly to ourselves."

However we remember them, our memories, even those tinged with touches of imagination, are unique to us. They make up the fabric of our lives and define who we are.

Brain stat: There are 100,000 miles of blood vessels in the brain.

The Casino Effect

Moments of creative inspiration which we feel we can hardly take credit for and which arrive almost by accident, are compelling reminders of the power of the brain. These insights might be rooted in the brain's visual and auditory cortices, but it is the association cortex which connects everything together and becomes particularly active when we are being creative.

An American product developer whose luck changed in the 1980s is an example of this. He went to a lecture given by scientist Spencer Silver who had recently invented a new kind of adhesive which was strong enough to attach pieces of paper together, but pliable enough to be separated and then re-attached. He was looking for a way of exploiting his discovery but had been unable to find an answer.

The product developer was Arthur Fry who sang in a church choir. Each Sunday Fry had noticed that the slips of paper used as hymn book markers constantly fell out. It suddenly came to him that Silver's glue would provide the perfect answer. By coating the paper with the adhesive, a reusable bookmark could be made without harming the page itself.

It seems that imagination and memory are firmly fixed together and each has a powerful effect on the other. Moreover, MRI scans have shown that using either sends blood to exactly the same areas in the brain. As an original thought materialises, the association cortex goes into hyper drive and while in this irregular state, unrelated thoughts connect in a seemingly arbitrary way. When this happens, the brain instantly and magically regroups and organises itself to accommodate them reaching a logical conclusion in the process. Like pulling the handle on a one-armed bandit machine, the numbers form into a winning line as in Fry's case - and welcome to the Post-it note.

Déjà vu

The French term, déjà vu, has an interesting and exotic ring to it until translated into English where it loses its edge. 'Already seen' sounds far too pedestrian for a feeling which might only last moments but is nevertheless extremely vivid. When it occurs, we may feel unnerved, as though we are looking in at an experience that we seem to have been a part of in the past and are now somehow reliving again. It's as though we have been transported into another dimension where normal rules have been abandoned. But why does this happen?

Psychologists studying the phenomena think it might be linked to a slight confusion within the brain's circuitry where the event is taken to be a recollection. The brain processes information about the present in such a way that it appears to be an experience from the past. The detail is so vibrant that the next moments can be predicted from second to second. Because of this an almost supernatural element creeps into the equation, the idea of 'otherness' and unseen hands at work, which also suggests that different circuits are responsible for memory and recall.

Statistics show that about 70% of the population have experienced déjà vu moments at some point in their lives but research has also shown it occurs most commonly among 15 to 25 year-olds. It is also known to be more prevalent in epilepsy patients, which hints at slight abnormalities in the brain.

The déjà vu experience is puzzling since there is no clear memory of when, or even if, it happened in the past. However, an overriding certainty that it did must rank it as one of the more eccentric aspects of the brain's perspective on time.

False Memories

If déjà vu is confusing, memory itself, by its very nature is open to fluidity and change. Emotion plays a significant part in determining how and what we remember and so does repetition. The holiday we took might become sunnier, the heartache greater, the play or film considerably better or perhaps worse than our original interpretation. Memories repeated over the years alter without us even knowing it.

In contrast to a déjà vu episode, confabulation is a neurological condition which occurs when imagination fuses with memory to create a wholly fictitious scenario. A memory of an event that never took place.

But how do these false memories come about? In a BBC documentary, a group of volunteers was asked if they had ever gone up in a hot air balloon when they were younger. An unusual enough experience and one they might have remembered, but no one did. However, the production team then went on to mock up individual snapshots of the group in a hot air balloon and pasted in an extra childhood picture of each one.

They then showed this to the group who, looking at the picture of themselves, were still undecided and unable to bring the occasion to mind. However, a few days later, a number of them contacted the pro-gramme to say they clearly remembered being in a hot air balloon. One woman could even recollect feel-ing scared. It seems we are quite adept at convincing ourselves something happened, almost wanting it to have happened, when in reality it never did.

Brain stat: T cells in the brain have an inbuilt memory that recognises previous infections we might have had. This helps our immune system to go into action against new invaders.

Misinformation

If someone told you they could generate a completely false memory in a person's mind by using a simple recipe of suggestions and prompts, would you believe them?

In her research Dr. Julia Shaw, a memory scientist and criminal psychologist, did just that by creating a state of 'misinformation' by convincing people that something had taken place (in this case, a crime) when it actually hadn't. The idea of confusing imagination with memory and implanting powerful but false memories proved unexpectedly easy and showed how open to suggestion our recall system can be.

By concocting a precise recipe which involves a 'trusted professional' to mix the ingredients, adding one tub of social pressure, a large cup of falsehood and just enough reality to bind the whole lot together you have the perfectly fabricated memory cake.

For the brain, attempting to identify which ingredient in the final mix was false becomes extremely difficult since it will recall the false memory using the same neurons that it would with a true one.

Astonishingly over 70% of the students taking part in this experiment formed these false memories. The research concluded that the divide between real and false events and the memories they produce are much narrower than we imagined.

The Fame Game

Memory can be affected for the most unlikely reasons. In the 1960s Andy Warhol remarked that, "In the future everybody will be famous for fifteen minutes." Maybe he got it wrong. For many it turns out to be an even shorter period of time.

Our preoccupation with fame and the belief it has something substantial to offer filters easily through into our everyday lives; but memories are short when it comes to remembering who won last years I Wanna Be a Celebrity competition. The list of young hopefuls who disappear without trace is endless. Who remembers them?

But occasionally the fame game produces an unusual type of personality disorder in celebrities which can become powerful enough to affect their memory. It's known as known as ASN - Acquired Situational Narcissism - and results in a self-obsession that puts Narcissus in the shade.

When well-known personalities become over glorified and made to feel out of the ordinary, notions of superiority are often reinforced by the people around them who help strengthen their intrinsic narcissism. In the 1940s film Sunset Boulevard, Norma Desmond, the aging movie star character played by Gloria Swanson, displays typical symptoms of this condition. She deludes herself into believing she can resurrect her career and make a successful come back. Given her age, the odds are stacked heavily against her, but others are drawn into her fantasies and find themselves colluding in the deception.

The American actress, Winona Ryder might also have been suffering from ASN when she was caught stealing from a shop in Beverly Hills in 2001. The store detective who stopped her as she was leaving asked why she had failed to pay for the goods in her bag. Her reply? That she was rehearsing for a role in a new film and the director suggested that she shoplift for a role she was working on. In this case ASN meant she had presumed she was exempt from the normal rules.

With ASN, the person's sense of entitlement becomes so intense it disrupts their everyday life and how they deal with the outside world. It can also affect memory. Dates are missed, engagements broken and appointments forgotten, since for the sufferer, there is always something more pressing to attend to - themselves. Victims experience illusions of grandeur laced with arrogance which become so intense they continually place themselves centre stage under the misguided belief that they are the only ones on it.

After researching this unusual behavioural disorder American psychiatrists have come to the conclusion that these celebrities are not deranged fantasists but are suffering from an illness. They have, apparently, managed to find an expensive cure.

Flashbulb memories

As the name implies, flashbulb memories are ones hitched to events that are reported mainly but not exclusively in the media. The term seems to suggest an episode captured instantly and permanently, as happens with flash photography.

For the individual the term flashbulb also suggests an instantaneous and personal recall of an event. In that moment we remember the event but also see ourselves playing a focal role. The incident is significant but so are we and to that end we must be part of it in some way.

Often added details attach themselves to the picture and help bring the mental snapshots to life. Our experiences at the time of a major incident are then connected to the event itself and have equal resonance when we recount it to others. We, too, become part of the overall picture and feature in that important episode that took place in our lives. We clearly remember where we were when we heard news of a famous person's death, or international disaster like the 2004 Tsunami or the events of September 11th 2001. The unexpected resonance of these events, even though they might not have touched us personally, had a great impact which stays with us.

Recent research suggests there could well be a more pessimistic side to the brain. Scans of two areas where emotion is processed show greater activity when bad times are recalled than good ones, which might be the reason why flashbulb memories tend to hitch themselves to more calamitous happenings.

Coke vs Pepsi

The results of research on over sixty people who had their brains scanned during a blind taste testing of Coca-Cola and Pepsi produced surprising results. Although half the testers chose Pepsi and the other half Coke, in the test Pepsi tended to produce feelings in the prefrontal cortex, a region of the brain which deals with reward. When it was suggested to the Pepsi group that they had been drinking Coke, three-quarters said they liked it more. By contrast, during the Coke tasting, brain activity in the hippocampus which deals with memory rose significantly. So, consumers were choosing Coke not only because of its taste but because of their memories and experiences linked to the brand.

Inspirational Soup

Even in art consumer marketing makes its presence felt. We know   certain consumer goods stay with us whether we like it or not, but selling a copy of a Coke bottle and a can of Campbell's soup as art was something no one had thought of before.

Until that is, American pop artist Andy Warhol appeared on the scene, turned expectations on their head and drew attention to what art could or could not be. He produced images of ordinary, commercial products, called them art and helped initiate a new pop culture of the nineteen sixties. He realised that consumers, whether rich or poor, were in effect, buying the same things. "A Coke is a Coke." he said, "And no amount of money can get you a better Coke than the bum on the corner is drinking. All the Cokes are the same. Liz Taylor knows it, the President knows it, the bum knows it and you know it."

The public knew it as well and bought into the idea to such a degree that the iconic bottle has had a meteoric rise to fame. Warhol's glass contour bottle of Coca-Cola sold for just 10 cents in the early sixties. Fifty odd years later, however, his painting of the same thing sold for a staggering 57million dollars. There's really nothing like Coke!

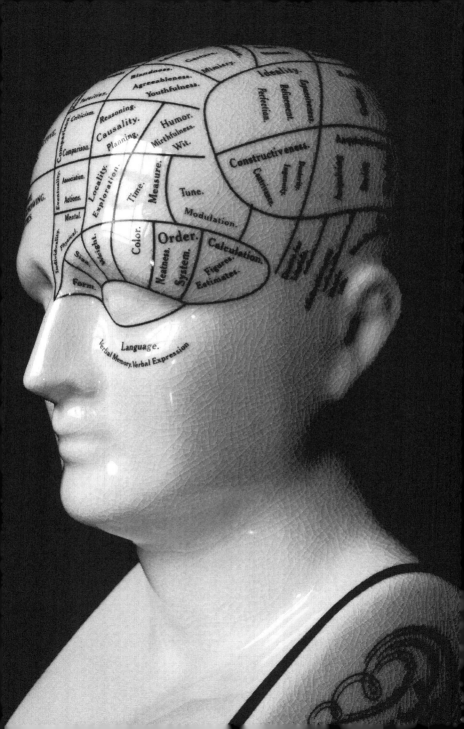

Mapping the Brain

Through the use of new technology and fresh ways of thinking, we are becoming more aware of just how vital memory is for human beings.

Back in the eighteenth century a man called Franz Gall thought there must be more to the brain than just a lump of grey matter inside our head.

He guessed that every bit of the brain must have a different function and came up with the idea of Phrenology. He reckoned that if he mapped out the various areas on a model of a person's head, he could show that one area was in charge of happiness another for jealousy and so on.

He also believed there was an area for memory, though here he went slightly off track by linking it to those people who had prominent eyes. However, with hindsight, Gall's work proved surprisingly close to the mark. We now know that each section of the brain works to different effect and conditions affecting emotions such as depression are treated by drugs that target only specific areas.

Given that the brain was virtually uncharted territory in the late 1700s, and no one could picture the inside of a skull let alone what went on in there, an instant and visible explanation of behaviour and character must have been exciting stuff. However, in the 1930s and 40s, the idea re-emerged in a more sinister way when the Nazis used phrenology measurements to check for racial purity in German citizens.

Although phrenology heads are now mainly consigned to museums and antique shops, Gall would be pleased that phrenology has remained with us on several fronts, not least by finding its way on to television in shows like the Simpsons as well as the American TV comedy, 30 Rock where one of the characters decides not to trust his boss because of a raised area on a section of his skull associated with deviousness. Some ideas just refuse to go away.

Brain stat: Your brain weighs in at roughly 1360g. About the same as lifting up a large bag of sugar.

Neuro Marketing

The days of marketing which connect our human senses with simple instant gratification may be numbered - sunbathing on a hot beach linked to a thirst quenching drink is an obvious example.

This kind of conventional consumer research might soon be overtaken as major brand owners look increasingly to neuroscience for reasons why consumers become engaged with products, allowing them access to our buying habits. By tapping into our brains and seeing how we react to certain products, they can modify their selling techniques more precisely.

It seems likely the powerful units of information known as 'memes' are responsible for influencing our choices when it comes to buying things. Dreamt up by the biologist Richard Dawkins in his book, The

Selfish Gene, a meme is a behaviour or idea which spreads through memory.

For example, lavatory paper folded to a point in hotel bathrooms has evolved into an almost universal meme. Once seen, it's a way of using familiarity to assure us and to fulfill the promise of a pleasant stay. Whatever their shape or form - a catchy tune we can't forget, a good joke, a fashion idea - we take memes on board, remember them, imitate them, then pass them on.

This new phase of harnessing science to sell products provides an opportunity to work out precisely why we are drawn to make a particular purchase in the first place. Techniques range from brain scanning to sophisticated online surveys. Portable EEG headbands are used by focus groups as they wander round department stores to keep track of the brain's reactions to each product.

Eye-tracking then links physiological reactions to what is seen. This allows the technology to pinpoint emotional responses to brands that we exhibit without even realising they existed. Later our memories will do the rest.

These new indicators signal huge potential for future growth. For example, a financial services company in the United States used these techniques to pick a new logo which reinforced memories relating to a feeling of trust. But at the other end of the spectrum a major food brand discovered that, whilst its consumers associated their logo with health and dieting, it also linked it with pressure and apprehension.

Paparazzi or Biographer

Increasingly a large percentage of photos taken are 'selfies' which now number over 100 million a day. In fact, over 350 million new photos are uploaded to Facebook on a daily basis - more since you read that sentence - and rising. That's a lot of saved moments to store. From President Obama and the Pope through to holidaymakers and party goers, this ensures the photographer is the centre of attention. But does the fashionable notion of a 'selfie' help us to strengthen memories any better than a standard photo or is it merely thinly disguised narcissism?

It's been said that a photograph is like a recipe - memory the finished dish. If so, do recorded images support memory more vividly than the brain or are they ultimately simply short term digital junk, a way of recording what you missed while taking the photographs? They are unlike personal memories of events which, without thinking we can edit, discard or save automatically to the brain's filing system bringing them to life as we wish.

At the 2014 Oscars ceremony, Ellen de Generes' famous 'selfie' included a host of stars and generated a record breaking one million re-tweets in an hour. Now we, too, can be the centre of our own self- styled Oscars' world, instantly recording our identity and adding sparkle to our memories in a way that may turn out to be less than satisfying in the long term.

Spool back...
Can you remember what ASN stands for?

3. EMOTION, MEMORY AND THE POWER OF SLEEP

"Can't put your arms around a memory
Can't put your arms around a memory
Don't try
Don't try"

– Guns n Roses

Can you remember the first time you fell in love with someone and how it felt? What happens exactly when we climb aboard that emotional roller coaster called love - when the heart races, butterflies dance in the stomach and the anticipation of seeing the object of our love again becomes central to our well-being?

Apparently, it only takes the blink of an eye for our brain to register all these emotions but the reaction differs according to what kind of love we experience. So, dizzy romantic love or long term emotional commitment, basic desire or just good friends; each can bring several wide-ranging responses.

Imagine you are going on a blind date. You arrive at the restaurant and the person you are going to meet is sitting at the bar waiting for you, wearing the distinctive green scarf you both agreed on and looking good. You walk up to them and smile but when they say, "Hello" you notice their voice is pitched oddly higher than you expected and their accent doesn't seem to go with their face.

Psychologists believe it can take as little as sixty seconds to decide whether or not you fancy someone and if love might follow. Body language plays a key part, as does the person's voice with tone, quality and pace leading the way. It's not so much a question of what they say, but how it comes across to you. Your blind date might quite possibly have had many good qualities and lots to chat about, but those initial fleeting moments of emotional connection are crucial for any positive long term outcome.

Falling...

Although we might remember details of when and who we fell in love with, in basic physiological terms the reasons why we might be attracted to someone are merely responses to rather unromantic sounding hormones such as estrogen and testosterone, which change our perception of the person standing in front of us.

In a study which scrutinised the brains of couples who had recently fallen in love, scientists noted that high levels of the neuro-transmitter dopamine - well known for triggering powerful blasts of intense pleasure - were released. This stands to reason, since doing what comes naturally is part of human behaviour and a drive for sex adds fuel to these pleasurable feelings.

A little later in the process, feelings of love are automatically strengthened with yet another hormone, oxytocin, which contributes to empathy and attachment in orgasm and is a key component in the bonding process between mother and baby after childbirth. Because of an association with compassion and its role in our need for touch and human contact, oxytocin has become known as the 'cuddle' hormone.

Ironically, although it increases our need for personal contact it is also responsible for feelings of jealousy. Coincidentally, a lack of oxytocin in people with autism is thought to contribute to their inability to empathize with other people and therefore engage in socially accepted responses and relationships.

This may go some way to explain the painful state that unrequited love can sometimes bring. If love is not reciprocated, we can become so distracted that other everyday thoughts take second place. Our focus becomes fixed on memories of the person who is the object of our devotion and what took place when we first met them. This one-sided state can lead to anxiety and depression and the memories of those first meetings are then amplified and distorted to the exclusion of rational thought, even by love's standards.

Memory plays a vital part, enabling the constant recollection of initial contact and emotional attachment to become central to our lives. Inevitably there will be no satisfactory conclusion and sadly, whole lives can be wasted on false memories of what might have been.

Even if there are moments of clarity about the inevitability of the outcome, this concentration on unreasonable expectations means that emotion has in fact conspired with memory to create a nightmare of delusion. Obsession with pop stars is an example where rational thought is abandoned. This adoration normally subsides eventually but in some cases it remains at a level which is both obsessive and damaging to other relationships and can lead to stalking.

Brain stat: The brain generates enough electricity to power a light bulb

The Prairie Vole

Of course, everybody hopes that love will blossom and, importantly, last. Here yet another hormone, somewhat similar to and operating in tandem with oxytocin, is working hard to reinforce the lasting quality that we expect from love. When scientists discovered vasopressin, a hormone released by the brain after sex which plays a part in long term relationships, they were involved in doing research into the prairie vole.

The love life of prairie voles is somewhat similar to our own, in that they indulge in much more sex than is necessary for the purposes of reproduction. They too, like humans, form relationships. But when male voles were given a drug that suppresses the effect of vasopressin, their bond with their partner deteriorated and they lost their devotion.

So, there it is. Love is merely a series of interlinked hormonal, chemical and electrical connections which can foster enduring human partnerships and can sometimes result in producing children. Our brain, it seems, is extremely practical in its orchestration of our feelings of love to gain this main objective.

But we also know that love can be experienced in countless ways. There is much more to it than that and certainly a great deal more than can be explained in merely physical and scientific terms. Is there any other emotion or activity which has given rise to so many songs, poems, paintings and movies, types of dress, perfume - in fact a limitless combination of ways to attract and retain a loved one - to love and be loved? Being in love can be all consuming, blind, irrational, unbalanced and often quite unpredictable. The effects of loss or gain are felt more strongly in love than in almost all other human experiences. Given the diversity of chemical reactions released by the brain when this is going on, it is hardly surprising the thing we call love is such a precarious and power-ful emotion.

Smell

Of all the senses we possess, our sense of smell is the one most often linked to memory. It's also by far the most personal and can jump start our thoughts in a way other senses fail to do. Unlike other animals whose world is governed by an acute sense of smell, ours by comparison is relatively undeveloped. For us the eyes and ears play a more important role in our lives. However, our smell and memory connections are strangely powerful and can capture the essence of places and people in an astonishing way.

The reason smells survive so well in our memory is because the stages through which they pass, rather like a combination tumbler lock, always lead back to the same place in our brain.

A smell can instantly catapult us back in time. The perfume someone wore, the brand of cigarette they smoked, a whiff of new mown grass on the breeze. Whatever it might be, a particular smell stored and remembered from early childhood can allow a feeling to take hold and replay the past in a matter of seconds. Suddenly you're there, jettisoned back in time and reliving the moment.

Smells are made from millions of minute particles moving in the air. As we breathe, our nose filters them through the nasal cavity until they reach the olfactory bulb, the centre of the brain's system for detecting smells. Each smell particle slots snugly into its chosen neuron which instantly sends signals directly to the brain where it's translated into the smoky smell of burning wood or the overpowering perfume of lilies. Perhaps this very close connection between the nasal area and the brain allows even the briefest sniff to become instantly hitched to a particular feeling.

Smell is extremely important commercially. For companies making washing powder the choice of perfume is critical. Keeping the same familiar scent allows the manufacturer to tap into our need to form an emotional bond by recalling memories of wellbeing. Imagine the smell of a towel washed in a favourite washing powder and put on the line to dry. When we hold it up to our face, the feel of it, combined with fresh air and sunshine, reinforces our experiences of comfort. Many emotions are triggered by scent - some not always pleasant.

There is a strong link between aroma and the enjoyment it produces. In tests carried out in a jewellery shop the added smell of perfume not only made a difference to how people shopped but encouraged customers to linger longer. Whereas in a factory, the smell of lavender released during a break at work, tended to boost flagging productivity.

Recently, various scents were even used to help diagnose brain disorders such as Alzheimer's and Huntingdon's disease. The diversity of smell, it appears, has no bounds.

Tears

When did you last cry? Was it through pain, laughter or sadness? Research has shown how a hormone called prolactin (which is produced less in men), gives women the edge when it comes to shedding tears. But whether you're a man or a woman tears are important for several reasons.

We produce three different types of tear. Each one releases different chemicals and hormones to cope with the various jobs they need to do; instantly varying their chemical makeup depending on the task in hand. Cutting up an onion, for example, is likely to bring on reflex tears. These tears contain less of the emotion producing substances and more of the basic variety we need to keep our eyes free of irritants. Onions release a chemical that upsets the surface of the eyes. To combat this, we produce the cleansing version of tears to lubricate and protect them.

It's often said that having, ' a good cry' has benefits. Medieval medicine believed crying was good for you because it carried away unnatural excesses from the brain. For some people crying is rare but for others it would be an unusual week without tears of some sort. Actors are well known for being able to cry easily. But this is a trick learnt by calling to mind earlier, sad moments in their lives. After a little practice they can cry at the drop of a hat and weep on cue. A useful tool when you are faced with having to sob every night in the theatre.

On a slightly more practical note, tears are also produced to protect our eyes from small dust particles which otherwise would damage the surface of the eye. They come from ducts situated under the upper eyelids and whenever we blink they create a salty glaze. Then they drain through more ducts on either side of the nose.

The French writer, Voltaire believed tears were the 'silent language of grief'. But they can also be an expression of happiness. A friend used to cry at least once a day, not because she was sad but because she remembered how beautiful the world was and felt that life was just too short.

For some people music can be an immediate tear jerker. As soon as a certain melody kicks in, suddenly and unexpectedly they well up and they find themselves crying. Another friend always howls when she hears Dolly Parton and Kenny Rogers singing Islands in the Stream. We have noticed it's the 'Ah Ha' bit just before the chorus that sets her off. Rather like actors who train to find a trigger, she automatically cries every time she hears it.

So, tears are good news, not only for lubricating and protecting our eyes but also as a sign of overpowering emotions. Crying seems to be a particularly human condition and as far as we can tell, no other animals release their feelings this way.

Brain stat: Each time a memory is recalled, new connections takes place in the brain.

Laughter

We all recognise the power of laughter and yet there seems to be no single area of the brain specifically dedicated to it. However, we do know that laughter provides energy as well as encouraging the release of endorphins, which increases our sense of well-being.

So, what makes this physical release an indication of happiness? When we hear it we recognise the emotion instantly and even listening to other people's laughter can catch us unawares and trigger our own.

Laughter is also linked to memory in a very obvious way. Anticipation of an unknown punch line requires us to remember how the structure of jokes works. Knowing what is about to happen and sensing that it will probably make us laugh, involves a complex series of brain activity.

In an experiment on the science of laughter, the brain was found to produce a pattern of regular electrical waves. Within 0.4 of a second of exposure to something potentially funny an electrical signal travelled through the brain's cerebral cortex. If the wave took a negative charge, laughter resulted. Conversely, with a positive charge there was no feedback at all. It seems the brain must first be caught off guard and through recognition of the likely outcome using stored memories, finally be surprised by the unexpected conclusion.

Laughter is not just for the moment either; apparently if you laugh you'll live longer, too. Research shows that physiologically we benefit from a regular giggle and absolutely thrive on laughter when it brings on tears. It not only lowers blood pressure but scientists believe the process of laughing can even boost the level of our immune cells and reduce stress hormones. As more oxygen moves around the body, muscles stretch and electrical impulses set off chemical reactions that release 'feel good' endorphins.

Laughter has also been shown to improve our ability to cope with pain. Again, naturally occurring endorphins are released which have a positive effect. The American author, Norman Cousins, suffered from a painful spine condition which made sleeping difficult. He clearly remembers how laughter helped him cope. Watching comedies on TV for ten minutes not only made him feel better, but the analgesic effect improved the quality of his sleep afterwards.

But for young mother, Claire Scott, laughter produces a totally unexpected side effect. Claire suffers from a rare disease called cataplexy. Whenever she gets the giggles they cause her to faint and she falls over. Sometimes she realises what is about to happen and can take action but at other times she simply collapses and blacks out. Laughter like this produces sudden weakness in muscles which varies according to the severity of the disease. It may cause weakness of the knees, or in cases such as Claire's, total collapse.

Research into humour tends to be less than hilarious and to analyse the reasons for laughter is probably to miss the joke completely but to people who study these things it's a serious business and even the darkest of subjects can produce the biggest laughs. Here are a couple of jokes to check your humour recognition and response levels.

Two hunters are out in the woods when one of them collapses. He doesn't seem to be breathing, his eyes are glazed. The other man whips out his phone and calls the emergency services. " I think my friend is dead!" he gasps."What can I do?" The operator says, "Calm down, calm down. I can help. First, we need to make sure he is actually dead." There is a silence, and then a shot is heard. Back on the phone the man says. "OK - now what?"

....

When I die, I want to go peacefully in my sleep like my grandfather. Not screaming in terror like his passengers.

The Power of Sleep

Maybe if we lie down our brains will work.

– from the TV show Seinfeld

A good night's sleep gives the body a chance to recuperate. During sleep the brain is washed clear of toxins and fresh connections are made. In experiments with mice, this 'wash' is ten times more effective during sleep. Research also shows that sleep and memory are firmly linked.

In one trial two groups of mice were given training in certain tasks. One group was then deprived of sleep. The difference between the two groups in learning and then remembering was striking. It appears that as the brain cleans itself, new synaptic connections are formed and this period is used to lock the previous day's memories into place, which ultimately promotes learning. The mice that slept made many more connections between neurons. This suggests that no matter how hard you train during the day, without deep sleep you can't form secure memories and improve learning.

Sleep allows the brain to restore its processing power, much as a computer might, by ensuring unwanted information is discarded. The synapses at this point fire seemingly at random and the brain, in order to make sense of the jumbled information, produces what seems to be a coherent and logical sequence of events known as dreams.

Most of us dream and some of us can even remember a particularly vivid dream we experienced. There have been many attempts to interpret these night fantasies. The Greeks believed dreams gave unexpected insights into the future and were important for the prophecies they contained. Sigmund Freud realised their power too, and in his book, The Analysis of Dreams, suggested they contained inner truths which could be analysed to find a deeper meaning.

Whatever our own night fantasies might be when revealed, they can often hold great significance if not to the listener at least to ourselves. If we manage to remember our dreams long enough to repeat them, it sometimes feels as though another person is telling the story through us and our unconscious mind has taken on a personality of its own.

When we dream, the rules of reality are left behind. Dreams surface most vividly during the light sleep or REM (Rapid Eye Movement) period. What is apparent with these unconscious meanderings, as with daytime thinking, is how much we are able to forget. Some dreams stay with us throughout the day but no matter how vibrant and intriguing they are at first, most evaporate quite quickly, as if memory has no need of them.

Snoozing...

Mikhail Gorbachev did it, so did Henri Matisse. The actress Tilda Swinton actually volunteered to do it in public. So many well-known figures have done it over the years, it's probably about time the notion that snoozing is not useful was thrown out of the window. Now it's official. A nap in the afternoon does you nothing but good so long as it's for no more than twenty-five minutes. Any more than this and it might interfere with your night's sleep.

Research also suggests that neurons themselves tend to doze off when placed in front of the television for more than a couple of hours. The longer we tune in, the less likely they are to fire up. Two hours TV watching per day is about the limit and for people between forty and sixty years old each additional hour can increase the chance of getting Alzheimer's by 1.3%. Anyone for a game of Scrabble?

We now know that the quality of deep sleep at night is linked to an improvement in memory. When volunteers were asked to practice tracing images in a mirror in order to remember word pairs, those who had snoozed for a while beforehand accomplished the task better. Although the difference was slight, this new research should encourage us to take forty winks more often.

And Mind Wandering...

You might easily have experienced it yourself.
You're out for a walk, listening to music, or only
half listening to a conversation and then the mind
meanders and without quite realising what's happening, unconnected thoughts spring up from nowhere
and take on a life of their own. There's a name for
it - The Mind Wandering Mode - and it can affect
people in different ways. The brain frees up, decides
to recharge itself and returns with a new perspective
on life, a kind of home-made therapy. A bit of shuteye
can do the same thing.

Night Moves

Londoner, Lee Hadwin started doodling in his
sleep when he was four years old, mainly on his
mother's furniture, which didn't go down too well.
But when he carved into a family heirloom his
parents decided enough was enough and took him
along to see a doctor who diagnosed sleepwalking but
couldn't explain why it happened.

His artistic talent only comes to life when he is
asleep and he has no idea why this should happen. "I
wake up in the morning and whatever's at the side of
my bed is there." Lee's nocturnal scribblings continued until he was in his teens when they began to take
shape as recognisable pictures, some quite involved
and elaborate.

Although he has undergone tests, scientists have yet

to make out what stage of sleep he is in when he begins to draw. As he has no memory of doing them the clue might lie in some kind of memory trauma he experienced in the past.

Lee cheerfully admits he has no interest in painting when awake. He believes a lack of sleep and consumption of alcohol might be the trigger for his artistic endeavour at night, with, perhaps, some kind of sixth sense playing a part, too.

However it happens, over the last ten years galleries have shown an increasing interest in his art and his paintings have sold well.

Brain stat: The term, 'grey matter' is misleading. Only dead brains are grey, a living brain is a washed-out creamy pink colour.

Insomnia

In Britain at least, two thirds of us experience insomnia and rarely get the recommended six or seven hours we need. But during those times when we find ourselves awake in the middle of the night, remembering we are not alone can comfort us.

Figures suggest that we are sleeping less today than we did 100 years ago - an amazing 20% less. While some of us resort to taking a sleeping pill, others are wide-awake and buzzy, reading books, listening to the radio and playing on ipads. But taking your Smartphone to bed may not be such a good idea.

Computers as well as mobiles can be the cause of sleep deprivation. Our reliance on them is such that over 70% of us feel unable to switch off and are still using them shortly before we go to bed. To compound the situation the blue light they emit is also detrimental as it suppresses the hormone melatonin, which encourages us to sleep. So, if we don't want to find ourselves wide awake in the dead of night, maybe we should try and wean ourselves off our much-loved hi-tech devices, especially before we go to bed.

Take a look at Gary Turk's video Look Up.
https://www.youtube.com/
watch?v=Z7dLU6fk9QY&app=desktop

Can you remember the last time you had a really good night's sleep?

We usually spend at least one third of our lives sleeping and when the pattern is broken for any reason it can be seriously unsettling. Statistics show that twice as many women as men find themselves awake at night. But whatever sex you are, a lack of sleep creates its own problems.

Apart from serious medical conditions such as diabetes, heart problems and obesity which are affected by the immune system's need for the 'repairing' action of sleep, memory is also affected. Our ability to fully concentrate, use working memory and retain information is dependent on sleep. In one experiment two groups - one sleep deprived and the other fully rested - were both asked to remember a single word. When the word was later seen in a jumble of other words, the sleep deprived group's capacity to remember was down by 38%.

While we are asleep our unconscious mind reviews the previous sixteen hours somewhat like a camera might replay a video. It firms up on the day's events and sorts through the actions and achievements that took place which goes some way to aiding our memory. This particular type of memory works better for some of us than for others but is thought to be caused by what is called, 'spindle' activity during sleep. These spindles are short high frequency bursts of electrical activity in the brain reflecting the transference of memory from the hippocampus - a vital area in the construction of memories - to the firmer consolidation based neo-cortex. This might help us understand why a particular name we failed to remember one evening, comes to mind the following morning.

Sleep also allows neurotransmitters to rest and regain their capacity for rapid-fire connections. But the correct rhythm between sleep and wakefulness also plays a vital part in allowing the brain to replenish itself and function properly for the wellbeing of the whole body. Of course, the brain, a permanent insomniac, never sleeps.

Spool back...
Can you remember which animal has a love life somewhat similar to our own?

4. DRUGS AND MEMORY

"The mind is like a parachute.
It doesn't work if it's not open."

– Frank Zappa

Cognitive Enhancers & Smart Drugs

From the morning cup of coffee in Manhattan to
the chewing of coca leaves in the Andes, there is
nothing new in a desire to change your outlook on
life with some mood-altering substance.

Each day, through the enjoyment of food, or by
drinking alcohol, or even tea, our mood is altered.
The brain seems to detect and then react to a favourite food, improving our state of mind and allowing
a sensation of well-being in a single mouthful. It is
this ability to react so positively to stimulants that has
prompted experimentation to alter the brain's natural
rhythm through drugs.

The idea of augmenting life's experiences is as old
as history itself. From at least the fourteenth century
onwards, we know the poppy seed derivative, opium,
was taken for recreational as well as medicinal
purposes. Many novelists, poets, painters and musi-
cians hoped to find inspiration under its influence,
but whether or not it actually improved the brain's
capabilities, or merely felt as though it did, is open to
question.

We are aware that deficiencies caused by certain substances can result in alteration in emotional and cognitive balance. As so often happens, science took a leap forward when prescription drugs, in combination with naturally occurring chemicals in the body, were found to enhance the brain's capabilities even further. These ground-breaking drugs modify the performance of the brain by changing its natural processes, and their value is now widely accepted and has been used to increase capabilities in selective areas of work and play.

The relatively recent use of 'smart drugs', so called because they quite literally smarten students up in the run up to examinations, is on the increase and has added an extra dimension to the concept of brain enhancers. The adaptability of Modafinil, for instance, originally aimed at combating cases of narcolepsy or extreme tiredness, is now proving extremely effective in boosting memory and increasing concentration during stressful times at work. Drugs such as Ritalin, developed to combat attention deficit hyperactivity disorder (ADHD) are taken by non-sufferers to alter their brain function. Controlled doses stimulate the nervous system making individuals more alert, better focused, and thereby increasing their overall performance. Research has shown that over 15% of students in some universities in the United States used Ritalin to enhance performance.

A survey of nearly 1500 adults found that one in five had taken Ritalin, Provigil (Modafinil) or beta blockers, to heighten concentration and memory. It's hardly surprising that the use of 'smart' drugs is on the increase. Why not maximise the potential we know is there?

We modify our lives around our sleep patterns and the day to day balance is disrupted if we lose a night's sleep. But cognitive enhancers allow us to function as normal after being awake for forty-eight hours or more. In the future, it may be routine to radically alter our sleep patterns simply in order to suit the lifestyles we wish to have or need. An ability to stay awake for longer than normal could be a bonus for people who keep unsociable hours doing shift work, or transatlantic competitors sailing at night.

In the UK alone, 1 in 6 people suffer from a psychological or psychiatric condition. Until fairly recently, any adjustment to the brain's normal function, either through drugs or surgery was only likely to be used to correct a medical condition. In Parkinson's Disease, when balance is affected and muscles become inflexible because of low levels of dopamine in the brain, drug therapy can help treat the symptoms by boosting the flagging neural pathways affected and restoring some normality for a time.

Yet chemicals, such as dopamine, which is depleted in Parkinson's Disease, can also be instrumental in orchestrating mood in a normal brain by controlling our reward and pleasure centers. Raised levels can produce 'highs' of well-being, and, when bound with other naturally occurring chemicals known as endorphins, can produce some relief from pain. When this happens levels of dopamine increase and the 'feel good' factor takes over. This is why soldiers continue fighting after they have been wounded, and why runners overcome feelings of tiredness and pain and instead experience 'runner's high'. Daredevil sports such as big wave surfing, cave diving and base jumping can also create the same feeling.

This 'feel good' dopamine rush might also be experienced in other circumstances; doing a heavy 'work out' in the gym, for instance, or a long run, laughing, having sex, or even eating our favourite spicy food. Chillies contain an ingredient called capsaicin which leaves a 'hot' feeling in the mouth. While eyes smart and we wipe away the tears, a reaction takes place in the body which triggers the release of our own endorphins and makes us feel good.

Benefits

All this has prompted debate as to what degree these new drugs help facilitate memory and for how long. Scientists have yet to fully understand precisely how the drugs work in the brain in order to boost performance skills. They will not, however, turn us into whiz kids overnight. Even though increased performance may be desirable, what if the drugs were not available? Would the recently enhanced brain then fall back to the previous natural performance level or perhaps, alarmingly below it? Drug enhancement in sport, for instance, whilst being illegal, has been known to give an unfair advantage to participants, and many people believe that altering the function of the brain is the underlying reason.

Vision and Light

It's difficult to believe but every colour we've ever seen throughout our lives actually begins with just three - red, green and blue. But when it comes to light catching the eye, chartreuse, an acid yellowy green pigment, activates more brain receptors to fire than any other colour.

Our brain then unravels that colour information via the retina, where millions of photo receptors called cones work out the precise colour wavelength of the light they see. The cones then feed the information to the visual cortex and any subtle variations are seen as colour and tone. A red tomato is absorbing all the light that hits it, except at the red end of the spectrum.

So, it's red light that reaches the retina. Importantly, colours are also connected to our memory of the shape and size of any object. In this case the brain then interprets the whole result as a tomato. Although if the brain was to be confronted with say, a yellow tomato, then memory would come to the rescue and we would still recognize the object as a tomato.

Brain stat: Albert Einstein's brain was smaller than average (1360g) weighing in at 1230g

Home Made Colour-Coded Combinations

One of the short term and dramatic effects of drugs such as LSD and cannabis is an altered perception of colours which appear brighter and more intense. A version of this psychedelic effect, popularised in the 60s, where colour intensifies, also occurs quite naturally in a condition called synaesthesia. This is where the senses blend together allowing one sensory system to spill over into another. The overlapping of certain sensory circuits allows information to be sent to two places at once and triggers a response in other neighbouring senses - a sort of blurring at the edges effect. Any sensory combination is possible, but the most usual mix involves coloured letters and num-bers, although sound and smell can occasionally be involved.

Letters and words become visualised and in colour. For example, the letter R might appear as blue, while the number 8 is light orange. Words, too, might take on colour. Monday's a deep red perhaps and when someone's name is associated with a colour it will often be remembered as the colour rather than the name itself.

Taste buds can also be affected by music, so when listening to a favourite track the sensation of tasting popcorn can be simultaneously induced. Scientists believe these unusual connections could be genetically driven, as they appear to happen auto-matically in those people who experience them, and once set remain so forever. Many variations occur in synaesthesia but imagine what it would be like if our memory was enhanced by colour and we were able to link up with a world of technicolour reminiscences.

One of the first accounts of someone with synaesthesia was recorded by the philosopher John Locke at the end of the seventeenth century. He was baffled when, out of the blue, a blind man informed him that he experienced a scarlet, red colour whenever a trumpet played.

In fact, the notion of music being hitched to visual art goes back to Plato's time when he suggested there might be a link between harmony and art. It's believed that the composer Ludwig van Beethoven saw B minor as the black key and D major as the orange key. And why not, after all, the colour spectrum is graded in a similar way to musical octaves.

People with synaesthesia occur more frequently than we might imagine. The American movie star Marilyn Monroe was thought to have it and in Norman Mailer's biography of her he said, "she has that displacement of the senses which others take drugs to find."

On the other hand, for the jazz pianist Duke Ellington, the colour of musical notes changed according to who was playing them. "I hear a note by one of the fellows in the band and it's one colour. I hear the same note played by someone else and it's a different colour. Colour also played a part in singer/songwriter Jimi Hendrix's music and his famous 'purple chord' was used in the song, Purple Haze.

So perhaps, when you hear a guitar being played

you feel a slight itch on your elbow, or if you are absolutely sure Saturdays are a deep green, you, too, might have synaesthesia. But even if our memories occasionally appear slightly rose tinted, research has yet to come up with someone whose memories are tinged with a deeper shade.

Brain stat: the brain doesn't feel a thing. It has no pain receptors.

The Brain Drain

The concept of untapped or underused areas of the brain - up to 90% -has intrigued scientists for some time. This debate came about when neuroscientists in the early 1900s misunderstood exactly what proportion of nerve cells were firing at any given moment and concluded that large areas must lie dormant.

But now advanced brain imaging techniques such as magnetic resonance imaging (MRI), give us a clearer window into the workings of the brain and its areas of activity and prove conclusively how efficient and finely wired the system is. The notion, therefore, of unused 'silent' regions would appear unlikely.

In 2010, the Discovery Channel's science entertainment programme, MythBusters, put the 'only 10% use of the brain' myth under scrutiny.
A contributor was asked to carry out a complex mental task while hitched up to a MEG device, which tracks electrical charges in the brain. The machine

showed that a great deal more than 10% of the brain was involved in performing the assignment.

Spool back...
Can you remember what special ingredient chillies contain?

5. SUPER MEMORY

*"There are lots of people who mistake their
imagination for their memory."*

– Josh Billings

Being able to fly or have incredible strength or even
X-Ray vision may be many people's dream of pos-
sessing Superpowers - where they actually become
like Superman. Countless stories in books and films
have tapped into this most elemental human desire
where fate takes a hand and you acquire amazing
extra-terrestrial strengths.

In fact, the reality is almost as bizarre as the fiction.
Some individuals do seem to have phenomenal other-
worldly powers in addition to their normal human
abilities.

Kim Peek, best remembered as the inspiration behind Dustin Hoffman's character, Raymond Babbitt,
in the film Rain Man, was a mega-savant. Techni-
cally, savant syndrome means having an unusually
profound and complex depth of knowledge in a
particular skill but in Kim Peek's case his ability to
store information was truly outstanding. Unlike other
savants, he had a super photographic memory not
only in one area but in subjects as diverse as litera-
ture, music, science and maths. Imagine logging,

remembering, and then having the ability to recall the entire list of postcodes, area codes and road numbers of every single state in the USA. If that wasn't enough, this staggering ability stretched to memorising thousands of books, too. But why was his photographic memory so prodigious?

For most of us, the right and left side of our brain are joined together by a small strip of membrane called the corpus calossum. Kim Peek was born without one and therefore any information he took on board was able to flow freely between the two sides. This unusual condition also allowed his eyes to work independently of one another and although it might be difficult to imagine this, he could read the left and right pages of a book at the same time. Like a human database, huge amounts of information could be taken on board in this way and at breakneck speed.

For Peek, his extraordinary ability began soon after he was a year old. At six he decided to memorize the Bible and succeeded. On average, it took him only about an hour to read a book. Instead of using an abacus to help with adding and subtracting, he used the columns in the telephone directories to help test his mental arithmetic. Amazingly, his recall of everything he logged was also instant. Inevitably, these remarkable capabilities drew comparisons with the way a computer operates and his astonishing talents never left him. The older he got the more he managed to remember.

Unfortunately, this superpower had its downside. Peek was often sidetracked and found it difficult to perform some of the more basic tasks we take for granted. Fundamental things like cleaning teeth, washing hair or laying the table were beyond him. He didn't master the art of walking until he was four years old and was in his teens before he could climb the stairs.

Superpower - Perfect Recall

Russian born Solomon Shereshevsky became a journalist in the 1920s and could remember practically everything that happened to him throughout his entire life. Whenever he was given an assignment at work he never wrote anything down. His editor noticed this and at a meeting they both attended asked him why he never took notes. To everyone's amazement he proceeded to recall the meeting word for word and was surprised that they were unable to do the same. He was sent to a psychologist who diagnosed synaesthesia but in a rare and complex form. For Shereshevsky, it wasn't merely a question of colour-coding letters and numbers. With him, the stimulus of one of his senses affected all the others.

Unfortunately, the raft of mental images he conjured up could be so intense it created problems. On one occasion he wanted to buy an ice cream and asked the lady serving him what were the different flavours available. The tone of her voice when she told him they were fruit ice cream was such that he immediately pictured black cinders pouring out of her mouth. Upset by this distracting image he found himself leaving the shop empty handed.

At one point, Shereshevsky wrote down and burnt the memories he wished to forget in the hope that by watching them disappear in a puff of smoke, he would finally erase them from his mind. Throughout his life his incredible recall left him with a sense of frustration. He felt he was capable of accomplishing more and he wanted to be remembered as a worthwhile achiever. Sadly, he felt he had never quite reached his true potential.

Superpower - The Human Camera

The artist Stephen Wiltshire was diagnosed with autism when he was three years old. This particular condition, combined with an extraordinarily heightened visual memory and artistic flair, created an exceptional drawing talent.

He can look at a scene or building just once and his memory can store an accurate picture which he can then recall and replicate perfectly. Every detail will be perfect with no extra embellishment; every last parapet, curve and brick is correctly positioned.

This incredible artistic ability has allowed him to produce the most complicated and intricate drawings and to visualise a three dimensional, solid building even from a photograph, with absolute accuracy. He has been called, 'a human camera' but his pictures are far more than mere replications of a given scene. First and foremost, he is an artist who combines accurate detail with artistic flair, bringing his own individual style to whatever subject he chooses.

Over half a million people in the UK suffer from autism and of these around 10% will be savants and in the general population this figure is about 1%. It has a strong genetic basis and affects the way nerve cells in the brain process information, which in turn leads to unusual behavioural patterns.

Like many of those who suffer from autism and have difficulty interacting with other people, Stephen barely spoke until he was seven years old but the one thing that did make sense to him as a child was drawing with paper and pencil.

Superpower - Highly Superior Autobiographical Memory

Jill Price from Southern Californian, when describing how it felt to have an abnormally strong memory says, " Most have called it a gift. But I call it a burden." Since she was fourteen years old she has been able to recall every moment of every day in her life. Mention any date and immediately images flow through her mind ranging from what time she got up to what she ate and exactly what she did throughout that day. "I have a running movie in my head that never stops. There's always a whisper in my ear," she says.

Scientists are still unsure what's going on in the brain when these connections happen and strangely, this type of memory which enjoys such excellent re-call has more to do with not being able to forget than being remarkable at learning or intelligence.

For Jill, the emotional impact is totally draining. Not only does she recall the facts as they happened, but the emotions that went with them also return to her. Many of them are happy, but the painful ones linger and intrude into her everyday life.

Jill has no choice but to remember everything and her dairies show just how accurate her memory is. Yet the burning question of how she does it remains.

The condition is extremely rare but Hyperthymestic Syndrome and Highly Superior Autobiographical Memory (HSAM) as they're known, have doctors baffled. Price shares her condition with a handful of others worldwide who also share a common but strangely similar compulsion. They collect old movie guides and theatre programmes.

Brain stat: 70% of the body's glucose is burned up by the brain.

Superpower - The Knowledge

If you want to drive the iconic London black cab even in the age of sat navigation systems, you need to pass 'The Knowledge' to get a licence. The exam not only requires would-be taxi drivers to immerse themselves in over 300 routes in the city, but 25,000 streets and countless landmarks as well. This huge amount of learning appears to cause structural changes in the brain, resulting in, among other things, an enlarged hippocampus.

Dr Eleanor Maguire, Senior Research Fellow at University College London, discovered this phenomenon when she scanned the brains of over a dozen taxi drivers who had passed The Knowledge. Her findings showed they all had a larger than average right side to the hippocampus, suggesting that spatial memory - the memory we use to get us from A to B - is stored in this, our own personal sat nav area of the brain.

Superpower - Motivation

Entering the World Memory Championships is certainly not for dummies - but curiously it's not for geniuses either. Even when contestants' brains were scanned nothing was found in the structure to be out of the ordinary. It's all down to practice. So not so much about how brains are wired but how their owners train them. And the more they practise the easier it gets.

Alex Mullen, medical student and the 2015 World Champion explains, "Everybody has this ability built in even though most people will tell you they don't have a great memory. I didn't either." That is until he discovered a book called, Moonwalking with Einstein - The Art and Science of Remembering Everything by Joshua Foer. "My memory improved pretty much instantly. I use the same kind of strategies in medical school, it's like I'm cross-training for the memory competitions."

Mullen can remember how 52 cards in a deck are arranged in under 29 seconds which means memorising a series of 615 digits in order. He can also remember the precise order of 102 digits after hearing the sequence only once.

However, if you find it difficult to remember a shopping list or what you were doing last Thursday, don't be too hard on yourself. Interest is one of the prime connectors to having a good memory. That and a healthy dose of curiosity makes remembering anything much more likely.

Spool back...
How many people in the UK suffer from autism?
Over half a million? A million?
Just over a million?

"One night, four of us were on duty. Twenty-four-hour stuff. We had one Sten gun between us. And the bloke on guard at the time heard movement nearby. Thinking it was an attack he used the gun and fired into the bushes, killing several camels by mistake. When Libya's King Idris heard about this he wasn't too pleased. Rather like swans are to the Queen, so were camels to the King. He came down hard on us and said we had to recompense for the dead animals. The air force had to pay up - about the same amount as a Standard Vanguard Pickup Truck cost at the time."

– John Keene,
RAF wireless operator
El Adem, Libya

PART TWO
CARE AND MAINTENANCE

6. WHEN IT ALL GOES WRONG

"Fortune, fame
Mirror vain
Gone insane
But the memory remains"

– Metallica

The complex puzzle of hedged pathways in a garden maze creates a game strategically designed to make it as difficult as possible for the person negotiating their way through to leave. A good memory and cunning trail settings can help locate the exit, but as each turn looks like the last, the impossible task of avoiding dead ends is more down to luck than anything else.

It's the same for our own memories, trapped in a web of neural pathways which refuse access. Although, unlike a maze, they are looking for a way in rather than out. As we search for that illusive name or place that fails to come to mind, the chances of remembering what they are seem remote until a while later, when they unexpectedly pop into our head. Hidden connections are made. We remember.

But statistics also show the importance of forgetting. If we find ourselves concerned about our ability to remember, our need to forget is equally strong. We remember automatically, without even realising we are doing so. Thoughts surface faster than the speed of light and a raft of unconscious actions which necessitate thousands of minute interactions constantly take place, most of which we are totally unaware of.

In fact, of all the information taken on board we are programmed to discard over 90%. If we hung onto it all without the ability to discard most of it we'd be swamped with irrelevant information and the brain would suffer an overload crisis which would hamper our ability to function.

Our knack of jettisoning information is so vital that during one of those forgetful moments it might cheer us up to remember there might well be a good reason for it.

Brain stat: A lack of blood supply to the brain for over 10 seconds will result in unconsciousness.

Amnesia

All of us are prone to forgetfulness but amnesia sufferers' memory failure is significantly more serious and is due to a malfunction of certain structures in the brain. It's the general term used to describe memory loss, either long lasting or short-lived, but it usually applies to the latter. The damage caused by head injuries, traumatic events and some types of drugs or alcohol can blank out past memories which need not necessarily be permanent and with time and patience can often return.

Interestingly, in the world of fiction, whether books or films, the effect on a character who loses his memory has proved an extremely useful script device for writers. In A Tale of Two Cities, Charles Dickens describes one of the characters, Dr. Manette, as having blocked out all memories of his appalling experiences imprisoned in the Bastille. Only later, as the novel unfolds, do certain recollections of the time he spent there come to light.

A different kind of memory loss occurs in the film, The Bourne Identity. Here the entire plot hinges on our hero, Jason Bourne, being unable to remember who he is. He discovers by degrees a gift for espionage, languages, and self-defense - all the attributes of a government agent. But how these talents were acquired he has no idea. They appear to him as mere facts, not memories, unlike the Dickens character who gains access to what happened before through his emotional recollections.

Whichever way a character unravels the past, especially when the audience or reader knows more than the person involved, it creates an added dimension and draws us further into the plot. For an audience, the fascination of this awful predicament seems to stem from the idea that any notion of self is linked inextricably to our memory and without these links we simply do not exist.

Dementia

We live longer now than ever before, and many of us keep working for longer too. So much has changed in the last fifty years that the suggestion that "70 is the new 50" is not unrealistic. Logically, we want to place emphasis on the physical aspects of our well-being. But, surprisingly, about 10% of us will get dementia at some stage in our lives and over 35 million people globally are living with some form of it.

The first sign that a person is suffering from dementia is usually some form of behavioural change, together with a difficulty in completing simple tasks, as well as the onset of confusion and memory loss. Perhaps the best known of the diseases that can cause these changes and lead to progressive memory failure is Alzheimer's.

Since it was first diagnosed in the early 1900s, Alzheimer's has been the most common condition associated with failing memory. Life expectancy at the beginning of the 20th century was considerably lower than today, and so death was not attributed directly to the condition. But with the increasing number of elderly people surviving into their 70s and 80s, Alzheimer's is now considered a major cause of death in old age.

More research is needed into a viable cure for Alzheimer's and there are some encouraging signs. The disease itself is complicated and not clearly understood. It attacks the brain by causing a build-up of abnormally shaped proteins which stick together as plaques and form tangles. These then block the normal function of the neurons and synapses that surround them, finally making that part of the brain atrophy.

Scientists are now studying the chemistry involved in Alzheimer's. There has been some progress in identifying immune cells that would normally protect the brain from destruction. In research on mice the process of brain atrophy has been halted with drugs, and memory loss subsequently slowed.

With this breakthrough, alongside other research indicating that certain modern cancer drugs show potential in tackling the problem of Alzheimer's, the outlook is hopeful.

Getting Lost

Can't read a map? As difficult as it might be for some, many people are wired with a marvellous sense of direction. Blessed with an inbuilt compass and a perfectly formed cranial satnav, they manage to tap into the ramifications of map reading with no problem. Others are not so fortunate. For us it's a foreign land, usually pictured upside down, where nothing makes sense and has little bearing on the town or city we are currently travelling through.

There can also be an additional problem. When visiting somewhere we can sometimes suffer from, 'topographical periodic memory lapses', or to put it another way - forgetfulness. You might have experienced this yourself. Arriving somewhere for the first time and marvelling at the beauty of the view, you realise later that you had actually been there before. Navigating a route from one place to another needs a whole raft of complex cognitive skills involving such things as decision-making, spatial awareness and memory.

In fact, we might learn something from honey bees who are clever at this kind of thing. In their world, a wonderful quirk of nature occurs. When wishing to alert the rest of the hive to a particularly plentiful supply of nectar they have chanced upon, they immediately return home to the colony to share the good news with everyone else. In order to do this, they perform a complex memory dance known as a 'waggle'. As with mnemonics, when we need to remember something we make up a rhyme or sequence of events in order to help the process, so with bees. But in their case the chosen method of memorising is through movement. There are also variations on the theme known as multi component waggles involving smell and mileage. So, a dance of about two seconds denotes a distance of roughly two kilometres to the site of the food store.

For the bees, the waggle not only commits to memory the nectar location but also allows them to pass it on to other bees. For the spectator bees, the directions received are so accurate they know exactly where the nectar is and what type of flower to go for and waste no time in buzzing off to find it.

On a more sobering note, after scanning the brain of a man who constantly got lost - even in areas well known to him, scientists in Canada found that he was suffering from SDTD (Selective Developmental Topographical Disorientation) an acute inability to imagine maps. A disorientation glitch many of us might be aware of to a lesser degree.

H.M.

The extraordinary experience of Henry Molaison, known as H.M. is often quoted by psychologists as it helped pinpoint the whereabouts of memory in the brain.

After a cycling accident in 1953, Molaison had an operation which doctors hoped would control the severe epileptic fits he had been suffering from ever since. The process involved removing part of the brain called the hippocampus. As far as the epilepsy was concerned the operation was a success. But at the same moment something else happened, something so unexpected his life was never to be the same again.

His doctor noticed that every time he walked into Molaison's room, he was greeted as if for the first time. If anyone were introduced to him, left his room and came back half an hour later, he would have no idea who they were. Molaison had developed profound amnesia and was unable to commit any new experience from short-term to long-term memory storage.

Even though the long-term memories formed before the surgery remained intact, he now lived a life devoid of any useful memory. Well-known faces became strangers, as did everything he came into contact with. What day of the week it was, for instance, or what food he had recently consumed. Each moment was completely new. It is almost impossible to imagine a life in which all the actions that take place on a daily basis are experienced as though for the first time. As he himself put it, "Every day is alone by itself, whatever enjoyment I've had and whatever sorrow I've had."

Later in the 1960's further tests were carried out. One of these involved making him draw a five-point star shape while looking in a mirror. Not an easy undertaking for anyone, but for Molaison it was extremely challenging, bearing in mind each time he practiced it felt like the first time. But he gradually became more proficient until one day he remarked that it was becoming easier. He had remembered practising the test. This meant he had some recall and scientists realised there must be more than one memory circuit in the brain. It seemed the hippocampus, which stored his declarative memory, was still functioning and subsequent tests proved conclusively there were at least two systems available for creating new memories. In Molaison's brain that area was undamaged and he became the crucial link in helping scientists understand how memory functioned.

Looking But Not Seeing

Our brain connects most readily with the things that affect and interest us. Advertisers recognise this when they produce TV commercials showing the value of a product we hitherto had not realised we needed or could be of interest. So, if we see a car advertised and like the look of it, we may then be prompted to take a closer viewing. But more than that, and crucially for advertisers, we will probably notice that model more readily when we see it in the street. The advertising concept is also helped by pleasant memories - sunny, open roads and good times, perhaps with a dash of humour thrown in. This type of extra prompting focuses the mind and by doing so helps us remember. It has proved to be a powerful advertising tool with close links to perception and how the brain handles information. "Haven't you noticed that new shop next to the market?" someone will say. "Surely you must have, you walk past it every day." Perhaps we did see it, but more likely the shop held no interest so we have forgotten it.

Examples are everywhere. The Selective Attention Test (http://www.youtube.com) shows that by suggesting what the viewer's focus of attention should be, the brain will generally concentrate on that alone.

Looking but not seeing allows the brain to discard unwanted information before it can be lodged in our memory. We can be visually scanning in an unconscious way without seeing and registering any detail. By contrast, looking and seeing is based on selective perception during conscious visual stimulation in which memory recall plays a significant part. So, next time you are hurrying along a familiar route, why not pause for a moment and look again.

Nicknames

Many of us are landed with nicknames we would rather not have. Nevertheless, they can be handy when it comes to triggering memory. The enduring appeal of nicknames is such that it is quite possible to remember the nickname of an old friend you haven't seen for years, while totally forgetting their real name. The sixteenth President of the Unites States, Abraham Lincoln who had an exceptional memory, once remarked, "No man has a good enough memory to be a successful liar." This, however, never applied to the infamous mafia boss, John Gotti. Nicknamed the Teflon Don because of his ability to slide out from some of the criminal charges brought against him, he managed to escape doing time in jail on several occasions.

Later uses of this nickname referred to Tony Blair as 'Teflon Tony' and president Ronald Regan was 'The Teflon President', although not for the same reasons. More recently, the 45th President, Donald Trump, was labelled Teflon Don by many in the United States who felt nothing, or perhaps nobody, seemed to stick to him.

Using a household product might seem an unlikely way to make a connection but it does. The connotation of the brand name Teflon sticks in our mind and makes it memorable, as does the name attached to it.

Brain stat: Given its size, it's not surprising the sperm whale has the largest brain. It weighs in at 7kg. Over 17lbs. However, the emu has a tiny brain, smaller than its eye.

Recognition and Repetition

The countless actions we use in our daily lives, whether brushing our teeth, sending a text, or tying our shoe laces, all require recall gained through repetition. The process of going over what it is we want to remember strengthens our memory links with a minimum amount of effort.

But remembering someone's name, which is something we have to do many times over, can sometimes elude us. Those more fortunate are blessed with a natural flair for putting faces and names together, others realise the problems involved in doing so and consequently give up immediately. For them, the occasional situation when a new name is remembered without effort is startling and triumphant.

But before we accept our poor performance at recalling information, it might be worth trying a simple exercise. It's the face of the person being introduced that triggers the name, so the next time introductions are on the cards, take five seconds and look carefully at the person you are meeting. You might notice a slightly tip-tilted quality to their nose, astonishingly white teeth or unusual eyes. Then, repeat their name to yourself a couple of times before striking up a conversation. You might be surprised to find their name stays with you.

Americans seem to make it their business to remember names. They pay attention during a first meeting. I remember being introduced to a woman from New York who used my name several times during our first conversation. At the time, I thought she was being very attentive, if somewhat overly so. The conversation went something like this.

" Hi there, Vanessa. It is Vanessa, isn't it? Now tell me Vanessa, where exactly do you come from in the UK?"

The conversation continued in this way for some time with the moments when my name was used becoming less frequent.

When I left she shook my hand and said, "Good to meet you Vanessa." In that moment I was able to reply easily, "And you, too, Karen."

The unusual way she repeated my name in the opening moments of our conversation had prompted me, unwittingly to recall her own name. Because of the attention she had given to mine, remembering hers had been highlighted in my own memory and gained in importance. So, 'Karen' effortlessly sprang to mind.

Brain stat: 1.5 pints of blood travel through the brain each minute

Sorry - I've Forgotten Your Name

You're at a reunion party and notice a classmate you haven't seen for some time. Even so you recognise her immediately. This type of recall is due to a small area of the brain with the unusual name of the right fusiform gyrus and it instantly kicks into action when we meet someone and tells us we know who they are.

No doubt you have experienced something similar. While this is happening another area of the brain alerts us to the fact that although she has weathered rather well and still has that distinctive mole on her left cheek, her hair has turned a steely grey over the passing years and she has put on a bit of weight. But in this instance, although the brain managed to clue in all these facts about her, it slipped up on one vital ingredient - her name.

Face recognition is a complex process and several areas of the brain are used in order to deal with it. The temporal lobe plays a large part in helping us to recognise faces but in the case of an old school friend it singularly failed to do its job. Although the face was remembered as well as other physical attributes, retrieving her actual name was a step too far. Recall wasn't up to speed and it let the side down.

Daniel, David or Don?

Unlike meeting an old friend from school after many years and having no idea of her name, the moment when someone's name is on the tip of our tongue, (anomia syndrome) but tantalisingly out of reach is far more annoying.

Imagine being at a party and the name of someone we have just been introduced to escapes us. We accept this sometimes happens. It's maddening but natural. But then someone we do know comes over and for some inexplicable reason we are unable to remember their name either. Introductions fly out the window, blind panic takes over, and the only way to avoid owning up is to bolt for cover.

A few moments later both names miraculously appear from their game of hide and seek and we are left wondering what made them disappear in the first place.

The reason someone's name might not spring to mind immediately is due to a variety of things. Perhaps the clues we encoded along with the name weren't strong enough to stick. We were bored by the meeting and would have been more likely to remember the name if the person was interesting to chat to or fascinating to look at. Maybe our memory sensed there was no particular interest in this person and let the name go. Why hang on to it? Or perhaps, in the moment of introduction our thoughts were side tracked and concentration wavered.

For the brain, the pressure to remember may be linked to the need to forget - a vital part of memory maintenance. In one experiment two groups of people were asked to remember pairs of words. Then one group was asked to forget selected words from the pairs. Later both groups were asked to recall the pairs of words once more. The second group, who had been asked to forget, found the process of recall infinitely more demanding. Their brains had already made the decision to remove the information and found it difficult to reverse the process.

If we then return to our party, the circumstances have a similarity. We didn't think it was particularly important to remember the person we had just been introduced to, so we began the process of forgetting. But when suddenly confronted with the person we do know, our brain assumed that one name will be easy to recall and the other not. The social pressure to recall an unfamiliar name transfers itself to the well-known name and we find ourselves confused and unable to recall either. Increased blood flow and extra oxygen in certain areas of the brain are exactly the conditions needed to create panic and those vital names are suppressed.

Brain stat: the brain is made up of 75% water

The Doorway Effect

The simple action of leaving one room and entering another can, as if by some magical process, actually affect our memory. Scientists call this conundrum the 'doorway effect', where the action of walking through a doorway can literally alter our ability to remember why we entered a room. Although this effect doesn't last and after a few moments most of us remember what we wanted to do, getting a magazine for example, it can still be disconcerting.

The cause, according to researchers, is a human tendency to channel different actions into well-defined compartments in our mind depending on where we are. So, when we change location, we shut down the memory of that location and instantly replace it with the new one. This change allows the circuitry in the brain to experience a difficulty with a short-term memory because the process of going through the doorway has managed to erase it, however briefly. The landscape of the previous room is now being overshadowed by the introduction of new visual cues in the new room and this affects our capacity to remember the original purpose for entering.

Curiously, the effect is not apparent if we remain in the same room. In this case the brain holds onto an established pattern of recognisable landmarks and all is well, our memory is not affected and we will easily remember our magazine.

Spool back...   Can you remember the name of the man with the initials H.M.?

7. IT'S NEVER TOO LATE

"If you want to test your memory try to recall what you were worrying about one year ago today."

– E. Joseph Cossman

It's Never Too Late

During our life-time it sometimes happens that some folders in the brain's filing system refuse to open as easily as they once did, while others allow the sort of random access we used to expect when we were younger. To make matters worse we never quite know which memory folder will remain firmly locked until it's too late and we are left searching for clues to help us out.

Of course, many people have extremely good recall, their memory circuits buzzing with high powered neurotransmitters. Physical wellbeing also plays its part. Some of us slow down considerably later in life, while others remain fit enough to scale mountains. However we approach this process none of us like facing up to those, 'I'm not so energetic as I used to be' moments. Fortunately, memory is mindful of these minor inconveniences and allows us to ignore them for long periods at a time. Absent mindedness is brushed aside in the certain knowledge that most of our friends are going through a similar phase. And as for those senior moments - well, for some people they can be quite amusing.

However, when recall falters it stops us in our tracks. We feel that certain links and pathways have been selected for us and we have no control over the outcome. In that moment we might find ourselves remembering an isolated incident from a journey we took, but not who was with us, or even the country we were in at the time. But if we say 'holiday' then, 'Majorca' then, 'Harry and Debbie', we should find a path to the incident in the bar on the beach. Although any word might produce the entire memory, we must search our own database by using single clues. If one route fails, we need to find another. As we piece together the various strands we invariably get a fuller picture.

Fortunately, the time when fifty was considered to be over the hill has long gone. A recent survey revealed that old age now officially begins at well over sixty-five. Many will tell you they feel happier than ever, do a great deal more and an increasing number have decided to become late learners or to use the correct word, opsimaths. This word used to be linked to negativity when learning at a later stage suggested there might be a gap in education, reflecting laziness or even stupidity. Today the opposite is true and the notion of learning something later in life is associated with a positive effect on brain activity and ultimately memory.

These twenty first century opsimaths try their hand at everything from cross country skiing and charity treks to scuba-diving and even piloting helicopters. An example of this trend is John North, a 93 year-old, who started studying again in his sixties and obtained a doctorate. He also added an MA for good measure. Being an opsimath isn't just for academics either. Betty Hiple, from Swayzee, Indiana, realised a very active opsimath moment when she took up skydiving at the venerable age of 96.

We might not necessarily want to turn ourselves into instant skydivers or academics but getting involved in something new helps on several levels. It stimulates and relaxes us, keeps us in a better state of repair and allows us to take our minds off ourselves - a worthwhile process in itself. It might also improve our memory.

Brain stat: It's impossible to learn from looking at the structure of the brain what kind of person it belonged to - a mastermind or fool

Diaries

The main character in a novel by Edith Wharton, 'Ethan Frome', opens with the sentence, "I had the story, bit by bit, from various people, and as generally happens in such cases, each time it was a different story."

Before the days when people could read or write,

the only way information could be remembered and passed down the line was from person to person through chanting, storytelling and singing ballads. Of course, memory played an essential role but handed down stories alter in the telling. Slight discrepancies mount up and by the time the story has been around for a while it becomes hardly recognisable. One answer to these discrepancies is to keep a diary.

For Samuel Pepys, 1666 must have been quite a year. And thanks to his diary entry of the 2nd of September we can understand why. He gives an extraordinary first-hand account of the Great Fire of London as it swept from Pudding Lane near the river, engulfing everything in its path and changing the face of the city of London forever. The diary has turned out to be an amazing record of the Great Fire and Pepys' memory of it makes incredible reading.

With all the choices of social media at our disposal, where every aspect of people's lives are up for grabs, the idea of writing a private diary might not at first glance seem an obvious aid to memory. But diaries give a unique snapshot of life. Written down by the person whose thoughts and emotions changed over time - that other self - diaries are a very personal way of keeping track of the past. Modern fictional diaries whether written about a teenage boy or a woman's love life, strike a chord with millions of us and jog memories of our own.

Keeping our own diary becomes a memory hard copy, something to keep for life. There are other unexpected advantages as well. It gives pause, a moment for thought and in today's world of quick fire

communication when it might be viewed as a somewhat unfashionable occupation, the notion of
writing letters by hand might easily come into its
own again. Whether it aids memory has yet to be
proved, but it may well do so. It definitely helps
equilibrium. Sending an email or texting are light
years away from the leisurely process of sitting down,
finding a sheet of paper and covering it with words.
There is a less rushed approach to writing by hand, a
different mindset.

Digital Amnesia

Our world is changing rapidly. So rapidly that
studies show our smartphones are morphing into
memory hubs and our dependence on them and
search engines such as Google, are causing us to
underuse our memory.

If you are a rememberer, it might have something
to do with wanting to tell someone else and not keeping information to yourself. But, if that information is
obtained via the internet, there is no need to remember in the same way and we throw in the towel more
quickly and discard it. This type of passive memory
has no substance, no memory trail and we forget it.
When we rely on a computer to access information
it can have a detrimental long term effect which im-
pairs memory development. Facts are easily forgotten
because we know they are instantly available again
should we need them. This reflects a decline in our
attention span which has fallen from twelve seconds

at the turn of the century to eight seconds currently.

It seems that many people are able to remember a home telephone number from when they were a child, but not their current mobile number. In fact, nearly 50% of those who took part in a UK trial had no idea what their partner's phone numbers were, while the under 25's felt that much of the information they used on a daily basis was stored only in their phones. Why bother to remember such details when the answer springs up at the tap of a button?

Forgetting is something we all do and something we need to do but there is a danger of losing our memory skills in the short term belief that retaining information will be done for us and remembering anything is simply no longer necessary. We are fast losing the art of practicing the skill of remembering, something that should be nurtured not lost. Learning by heart could well be the answer.

Number Chunking

When it comes to retaining a sequence of numbers in our head - telephone numbers are a good example - seven seems to be the maximum amount we can remember at any given time. Any more and our recall becomes faulty. In our daily lives choices are constantly being made as to which memories are abandoned and which are chosen for long-term memory store. Things like pin numbers and dates, or grid references to a map are needed only for as long as it takes to tap into our iPhone. But when our short-term memory comes into play to keep hold of these numbers it lasts for less than a minute before we have to refresh it again. So, if we need to use the information a few hours later, it's likely we will have forgotten it. That is unless we use 'chunking'.

In the 1950's, an American psychologist, George Miller hit on the idea of 'the magic number 7'. Miller realised that, by assembling digits, letters or words in groups and not stringing them together as one unit, they became easier to remember. Take a long telephone number - 02044849771. 'Chunk' the numbers together in groups. So for instance, 0204 484 9771. With a bit of practice and repetition they'll pass into our long term memory store and we'll hang on to them. The regularity and rhythm of the 'chunked' digits is the clue to its success.

The brain enjoys working with patterns and Miller's research showed that by 'chunking' numbers in this way they stayed with us for longer.

Mobile phones have removed the need to remember numbers - the phone memory does it for us. But if for some reason we lose our mobile or find ourselves without one, it's useful to be able to remember important ones, not least our own. It's always good to have a small data bank of numbers at the ready for moments when we might need them.

However, in that moment of forgetfulness when the tricks of the trade, whether it be chunking, loci, mnemonics, acronyms, or whatever, don't work for you, why not take a different approach? When introduced to a group of people simply explain you have a terrible memory for names and numbers but that faces stay in your mind forever. Far better to be pro-active about a certain glitch and own up to it.

Brain stat: A live brain is squishy soft. Think of soft butter or tofu and you get an idea of how soft it is.

Straight From The Heart

For the ancient Egyptians the heart was the core of their being, the centre of emotion, thought and, significantly, the soul. For them, the idea that memory materialised in the brain was not understood. Although they were aware of the importance of the brain and were the first to coin the word and also to write about it, they felt it had little relevance as far as memory was concerned. The heart was key and their belief in life after death meant no one would have any chance of getting there without their heart intact. In order to achieve this goal, great care was taken to keep it fit enough to travel.

The phrase we are familiar with today, 'learning by heart' suggests that since the heart is the symbolic centre of human feelings, anything learnt in this way will probably be stored forever with repetition being the key feature. This allows information to stay in the short-term memory for increasingly longer periods until it moves on to more permanent storage and hopefully remains there. The ancient Greeks had a clever way of ensuring any account of history remained as truthful as possible. Professional 'rememberers' considered the facts and collectively harnessed their memories so that an agreed version of events could be handed down.

Today, it's no coincidence that many of the nursery rhymes and times tables chanted at school, stay with us. We had no choice but to learn them and the drill involved in doing so made sure they stuck. Thinking back, many hours seem to have been spent chanting times tables but to what end? Maybe the odd occasion when someone asks what eight sevens are! If they do, it's a good feeling to be able to reply swiftly... fifty-six. Of course, we still learn by heart! It's a nifty way to remember.

Learning by heart has many advantages. If you've ever heard a best man's wedding speech delivered with notes and one done without, you get the picture. One is 'heartfelt' and the other one is often dull and stumbling.

The Oscars are another good example of speeches learnt by heart. Of course, actors are more likely to get it right but even so an acceptance speech always come across more confidently when remembered. And actors themselves - well, every word they say has to be learned by heart.

Memory Triggers

With so much information about the world via the internet at our disposal, when it comes to organising information that is specific to us we need a very different personalised locating system.

Take keys, for instance. Leave them on their own for two minutes and it seems they will wander off. For this situation we need an advanced search method in order to track them down. Of course, all becomes simpler if they are always left in a pre-determined place decided on in advance. This may seem obvious but by choosing a specific location, a frustrating and time consuming search is avoided.

But during those moments when there's not a second to lose and the house keys which were always kept on the hook in the hall decide, for some inexplicable reason, to go AWOL, a microchip tag could prove a real time saver. Designed by a French company, BeSpoon, when the tag is attached to keys, glasses or any other item, it shows you precisely where the missing items are via an app on your phone.

Some cases might not need such a hi-tech solution. For instance, remembering to take a pill each morning will always be easier if the tablet is placed near the toothpaste - problem solved.

Mnemonics

'Right Tight - Left Loose' and 'Spring Forward
- Fall Back' are handy phrases when it comes to
remembering how to tighten a screw or which way
to change the clock by an hour to give us daylight
saving time. And who doesn't use 'Thirty days hath
September...' when it comes to remembering which
months have thirty and which thirty-one days? From
childhood onward, these examples of mnemonics
have proved extremely effective.

The techniques used in mnemonics are done by
organising facts in a simple, rhythmic way to make
them stick. No internet check is needed. If you want
to remember the colours of the rainbow for, say, a pub
quiz night, just use the name Roy G Biv. Each letter
of the name stands for the first letter of each colour -
so, red, orange, yellow, green, blue,
indigo and violet.

The word Mnemonic takes its name from the
Greek goddess of memory, Mnemosyne, mother of
nine daughters by the God Zeus, who were born on
consecutive nights, so the legend goes. She inspired
artists and sculptors, Japanese cartoons, a perfume
and a raft of computer software as well. In a painting
by Dante Gabriel Rossetti she has long, crimped hair
and looks a bit drained as she stares uneasily out at
us. But, significantly, she's holding a small lamp held
in the palm of her hand to symbolise memory.

Simonides

It's hard to imagine a world without the printed word. Back then, a good memory was essential. Many elaborate mnemonic systems were used to help things along and one of the earliest was devised by the Greek poet Simonides, over two thousand years ago. One evening when reciting a poem at dinner, he was called away to attend to some business and in his absence the roof of the banqueting hall collapsed, killing everyone. The result of this catastrophe was devastating and many of the bodies were totally unrecognisable. On his return, Simonides found he could remember where everyone was seated and was able to identify them.

Later, realising his powerful visual memory could be put to good use, he expanded the technique further to create the 'loci' or, 'location' method of cueing information. This involves something we all manage to do quite naturally on a simple level with no mnemonic help at all. For instance, when we have been out to dinner and mention it to someone the next day, we can easily recall who was sitting where, as we tell our story. But when the story we want to remember happened a while back and isn't so attention-grabbing, we need added impetus to bring it to mind. The idea behind the loci method helps us do this by connecting people, objects or whatever it happens to be, to various staging posts located in a familiar place. Maybe the mirror, lamp, chest of drawers or a picture in the room. Then, it's simply a question of hitching what has to be remembered to each item.

So, observation plays a significant part in what we are able to remember and how we manage to hitch it to our memory.

Some methods might be rather more eccentric than others. A friend, who tends to forget where she parks her car even if it's somewhere she visits quite frequently, has devised a 'spot the land mark' routine. After parking she stands for a moment, looks around until she finds two distinctive landmarks nearby. When she returns she looks out for these clues and easily finds her car. This is a perfect example of loci in action. Her method worked well for a while until she was in a car park one afternoon twisting and turning the key in a lock which refused to open. She looked up and noticed a stranger running towards her shouting and waving his arms in the air. Although she had located what she believed to be the correct landmarks and a car was there - it wasn't hers!

Most of us will have a couple of mnemonics up our sleeve from school days when rhymes and songs were a good method of remembering facts.

In fourteen hundred and ninety-two
Columbus sailed the ocean blue,

The date of the first voyage of the explorer, Christopher Columbus has hung on like a limpet. So for those of us who need a helping hand when something we need to remember refuses to stick, mnemonics might well prove to be the answer.

Posture & Physical Exercise

It has been said that although we can't change our genes, we can give them a good run for their money. Good posture and the way we move make a huge difference to how we look and feel and how others view us.

The latest research proves just how pivotal physical exercise is to our wellbeing and how it boosts brain-power, which in turn affects memory. Statistics show that building up to a brisk 30-minute walk five times a week is enough and may also act as a natural anti-depressant. Researchers found that when people who weren't particularly fit undertook an exercise regime for a few months, there was an increase in blood flow to the area of brain involved in memory. Tests later showed how exercising stimulates a neuron-manufacturing protein in the brain called noggin, an old slang word for head, and this in turn is responsible for fresh supplies of neurons.

Neurologist Jack Kessler says, " We could take a mouse that's not very good in a maze, give him the noggin protein and make the mouse equivalent of a mouse genius, running circles around a normal mouse". The findings are relevant since the birth of these new cells, known as neurogenesis, is vital for memory performance.

Fortunately, there is no chance of overdosing on noggin by doing too much exercise ourselves. For the moment, however, we will have to wait until the next breakthrough to find out whether we too can run rings around each other.

Breathing...

"Take a deep breath", someone might say, before the start of an examination, job interview or meeting, "It will help steady your nerves." We often use certain phrases to help combat moments of tension, but why? When we are nervous, excess amounts of carbon dioxide in the brain stimulate fear and by breathing in more oxygen we are able to counteract this acidity and calm ourselves down. Normal brain functions are hampered when oxygen levels are low, so the more oxygen you take on board the clearer your thinking will be.

More importantly, memory works better when we are relaxed and since we are now on the road to becoming more aware, we might as well take the rest of our body along with us! Repetition and an attainable but strict routine are the key factors for exercise. Any exercise, however small, if continued every day over a period, will be more beneficial than a lengthy work out once a week.

Spool back....
Can you remember the name of the Greek goddess of memory?

8. MEMORY CHALLENGES

"The true art of memory is the art of attention."
– Samuel Pepys

The metaphor of the brain as a muscle which needs working on like any other is a good one and from the various trials carried out, the benefits of participating in memory boosting exercises are tangible. The increasing popularity of brain-training electronic games and manuals show that in the same way as we might load the latest software into our computer, doing the same for our brains will improve our memory.

But does the ability to solve tricky problems and work out complex puzzles necessarily spill over and play a useful part in day-to-day life? Even if we know our memory might get stronger if we involve ourselves in crosswords, Mahjong and Sudoku challenges, should we start doing them? If they're simply not our cup of tea, it might be worth remembering that it's quite possible to boost memory on a simple level by paying attention to the world around us in an active rather than in a passive way. We could use this as a good starting point.

The following ideas don't involve video games, crossword puzzles or brain-training schedules and they do require a bit of effort but they might nudge us into looking at things in a slightly different way.

Simple Solutions

Naturally the characteristics of individuals vary but the well-tried process of memorising makes for better short-term performance while increasing the benefits for memory in the long-term.

A joke, a verse of a favourite song, a recipe - once again the secret is repetition. Perhaps, those who are still unable to remember their mobile phone number might make a start and hammer it home through chunking until it becomes hard wired it into long term memory. When the number is requested it can then unhesitatingly be reeled off with no effort whatsoever. (see Number Chunking page 109)

'It Just Slipped My Mind.'

Having an extra trick or two up our sleeve to deflect memory stall can be useful.

For those unexpected moments when someone's name escapes you, take a leaf out of the actor Sir Ralph Richardson's book. He had a great memory for faces but was often unable to attach a name to them. When approached by an acquaintance he recognised in the street he would often grasp them warmly by the hand and, searching for the name, say, "Isn't it?...........Isn't it?...........Isn't it a lovely day!"

The inimitable impresario and author William Donaldson avoided moments of confusion when trying to remember someone's name by inventing inappropriate nicknames. Twinkle was a favourite and was used quite indiscriminately on both men and women.

Singers, too, have unusual techniques for when they forget their lyrics. The popular classical singer, Lesley Garrett says that when she loses her way in an aria, she simply covers it up by repeatedly trilling "aeioe" until she remembers where she is. Mind you, this might be more effective and less obvious if singing in a foreign language.

In the world of theatre and movies calling everyone 'darling' may seem a little over the top, but there is an underlying reason for it. The process of acting may only last a day, so when constantly meeting new people and then bumping into them later, names are often forgotten. A cheery "Darling, how are you?" is both friendly and gets rid of the "What the hell is their name?" dilemma.

Another strategy when introducing someone to an acquaintance whose name escapes you is to simply ask them their name. They may at first be surprised you don't remember it. "John." they say. At which point you say, "Yes, I know that - but I'm afraid I've gone blank. I've forgotten your surname." They will then oblige by telling you and the conversation will move swiftly on, getting you off the hook.

Alternatively, when you find yourself in an even worse position and when meeting up with two people and both their names escape you, simply hold your hands up and say, "Why don't you introduce yourselves, I've just seen someone I must catch before they go."

Food for Thought

So, you've forgotten where you left your glasses…
again! If you feel your memory isn't coming up to
scratch, have a go at this.

Listed below are ten pairs of words:

Soufflé   Air
Dice   Skill
Bicycle   Puncture
Eggs   Speckled
Dragon   Cave
Kitchen   Grill
Boat   Mainsail
Mansion   Folly
Clams   Shell
Engine   Grease

Read them through slowly to yourself twice, then
cover them up and write down the pairs you can
remember.

Soufflé
Dice
Bicycle
Eggs
Dragon
Kitchen
Boat
Mansion
Clams
Engine

If you remembered more than half, you did well. But if you pictured an image of a soufflé rising, a boat and a sail etc. as you tried to remember them then you will probably have put the pairs together more easily than if you simply remembered the words on their own.

The point behind the exercise is to show how creating mental pictures and then linking them together can help memory, even if only in the short-term.

In fact, we do this unconsciously, without realising it. Someone mentions eating clams. You might remember going to the seaside on a wet afternoon, eating some, not liking them very much and ordering some chips instead. Connections inadvertently lead to other connections.

Why not try another memory game?

Look at the words listed below.
angel   hall   plum
paste   chip   coin
lift   bun   pen

Now, without looking at the above, circle the same words below.

maze   angel   lift   fact
paste   bond   flute   set
shelf   hall   bun   stool
pen   spoon   coin   dew
money   plum   dirt   chip

If you managed to pick out more than half, well done!

Your Starter For Ten

Everyone's thoughts get lost now and again but even so, our memory has an incredible filing system. To give you an idea just how good it is, take a quick look at these -:

1. Who oversaw the development of the iMac, iPod and iPad?

2. Who started the Body Shop?

3. Which former rugby player once called the English RFU committee, " 57 Old Farts"?

4. Which pop group sang Back For Good?

5. What part of the human body is phrenology concerned with?

6. What is the largest organ in the human body?

7. Who designed the SS Nazi uniform?

8. Tim Peake was the first British male astronaut to go into space but who was the first British female?

9. Who originally came up with the marketing strategy 'a free gift with your purchase'?

10. What is a sextant?

If you didn't know who started the Body Shop, for instance, or which pop group sang Back For Good, your brain told you it didn't know straight away. There was no delay. Perhaps it was something you never knew or it could be something you knew years ago and then forgot. So the brain, realising the possibilities are enormous, is likely to make no attempt at an answer.

Have another go at the questions - but this time with a multiple-choice answer.

1. Who oversaw the development of the iMac, iPod and iPad?
a) Conor Pierce   b) Richard Branson   c) Steve Jobs

2. Who started the Body Shop?
a) Kate Moss   b) Anita Roddick. c)Anita Redway

3. Which former rugby player once called the English RFU committee, 'Old Farts'?
a) Will Carling b) Jonny Wilkinson   c) Mike Tindall

4. Which pop group sang Back For Good?
 a) U2   b) The Rolling Stones   c) Take That

5. What part of the human body is phrenology concerned with?
a) heart   b) brain   c) intestines

6. What is the largest organ in the human body?
a) the skin   b) the brain   c) the stomach

7. Who designed the SS Nazi uniform?
a) Elsa Schiaparelli   b) Karl Lagerfield   c) Hugo Boss

8. Tim Peake was the first British male astronaut to go into space but who was the first British female?
a) Heather Shearer   b) Helen Sharman
c) Hannah Shievers

9. Who originally came up with the marketing strategy 'free gift with your purchase'?
a) Elizabeth Arden   b) Revlon   c) Estee Lauder

10. What is a sextant?
a) A group of six instrumentalists?   b) An instrument used in navigation c) A six-sided figure

Answers:
1c   2b   3a   4c   5b   6a   7c   8b   9c   10b

More than likely you did better in the quiz with multiple choices. If you know it, you know it, but sometimes multiple choice answers can help and when we allow the brain to be prompted by way of several likely answers, we might remember the correct one.

A perfect example of how this works are TV quizzes with multiple choice options, where contestants are given an opportunity to realise the answer is lodged somewhere in the memory store and the multiple-choice options may confirm it. The brain is allowed to explore other routes to reach the correct answer by narrowing the possibilities. We know that only one answer is right, so the brain now has the simpler task of discarding information in order to decide on an answer.

Scrambled Up

How cveler msut you be to raed tihs?

So lnog as the frist and lsat ltteres are posetionid corcretly in a wrod, we can dcehiper the meniang bcuaese we raed the wohle wrod and not the idvindiaul ltertes taht mkae up the wrod.

Research carried out by scientists at Cambridge University indicates that reading is as much about recognising a pattern as the individual letters or the words themselves.

Once the pattern is identified, any word then becomes easy to interpret. But it is human memory that makes it all possible. Any code, Enigma or otherwise, must start with a set of rules which can be learned and therefore memorised and words are no exception.

To illustrate how short-term memory works, look at these six letters:

TASHKBN

Glance at them for a second or two

TASHJBN

Which letter changed?

Try it once more.

OPCQLHY

OPCULHY

For the next test, just look at the first two letters below then cover them up and repeat what they are. Move down the line and see how far you get.

TE
SQP
LAJXU
MBUTYLES
VFKPIVHOZD
PLBODCIHNGRE

Maybe it was easier than you imagined. There might have been a pattern involved that helped. Chunking 3 or 4 words together, perhaps.

Brain stat: Because of the brain to body ration, female brains are generally smaller than male brains.

Recall and Recognition Test

The Robbery.

At 7pm the girl turned right outside the tube station and began to walk home. The light was fading and some cars had already switched on their headlights. A red mail van stopped in front of the post box. A postman got out and began emptying the letters and as he did so, an elderly woman carrying a grey umbrella crossed the road and handed him her letters. Ten minutes later, as the girl turned off the main road into a side street, she noticed a man walking towards her. He was well built but not tall. He had short, blonde hair and wore a dark brown bomber jacket and white trainers. As he passed he tried to grab her black shoulder bag and when she refused to let go he wrenched it from her hands, pushed her over and when she screamed he swore at her, saying, " If you don't shut up I'll hurt you." He quickly looked through her bag, took out her purse and ran off down the road.

When a similar scenario as this was shown on TV the mugger's face appeared on the screen for a couple of seconds only. Afterwards, when two thousand viewers were asked to identify the man from a line-up of six and then to contact the TV station with their choice, 200 hundred selected the correct one. The other 1800 got it wrong.

Now answer these questions without checking back.

1. What colour was the woman's umbrella?
Answer:

2. Was she old or young?
Answer:

3. What colour was the mugger's bomber jacket?
Answer:

4. Did she yell at him when he took her bag?
True/False

5. The mugger said, "Be quiet or I'll knock your head off."
True/ False

6. Of the two thousand viewers to telephone in to the TV station after they saw the mugging, 1600 identified the right man.
True/ False

The first three questions concern 'recall' which involves retrieving previously learned information without the need of external clues. i.e. the colour of the woman's umbrella.

'Recognition', on the other hand, is more concerned with identifying previously known information with the help of external clues. In questions 3,4 and 5 it's all about whether or not the information is correct. Although the mugger's face was only on the screen for a second or two, 90% of the viewers identified the wrong man, which only goes to show how unpredictable our memories can be. Research has shown how susceptible memories are to external influences such as misleading questions, the stress of the moment and the suggestions.

Eyewitness testimonies play a vital part in providing vital information during a trial. Juries are likely to believe what appears to be a reliable account of what happened at an accident or crime. But details and descriptions of what actually took place aren't necessarily consistent with what actually happened. Memory can be fickle.

Brain stat: Albert Einstein reckoned the speed of light travelled at 186,262 miles (299,792km) per second. Brain messages travel between neurons in just one thousandth of a second.

Memory Expectation

The brain has a remarkable ability to become accustomed to certain stimuli and inevitably memory tends to respond to rules and habits that become firmly lodged over time. The following story falls into this category where memory helps shape a conclusion based on past experience and expectations.

A boy is badly injured in a car accident. His father arrives at the scene of the crash and travels with him to hospital. When the nurse sees the child in the emergency room she realises he needs an immediate operation and calls for a surgeon. The surgeon arrives and says, "I'm sorry. I can't operate on this child, it wouldn't be ethical because he's my son." What's the story?

(Answer on page 137)

Jokes

People will often tell you they're bad at telling jokes. The more likely reason for this is their inability to remember the whole joke or worse still the punch line. Most jokes have an intricate and precise structure which must be adhered to. So, apart from the laughter factor which cannot be underestimated, all the subtle and elaborate information that is built into a good joke is a pleasant way to exercise the memory. For a joke to work it must be memorised off by heart accurately with no deviation from the script. We should all have at least one joke up our sleeve and here are a few to test your stand-up skills - and your memory.

A woman rushes to see her doctor looking worried and stressed out. She says, "Doctor, take a look at me. When I woke up this morning I saw my hair was all wiry and frazzled, my skin was wrinkled and my eyes were bloodshot - I looked like a corpse! What's wrong with me doctor?"
The doctor looks at her: "Well, one thing's for sure, your eyesight's O.K."

****

Two cows in a field. The first cow says," What's all this mad cow business about, then?" Second cow says, "Doesn't bother me, I'm a helicopter."

****

A doctor says to his patient," I have bad news and worse news".
"Oh dear," says the patient, "what's the bad news?"
The doctor replies, "You only have 24 hours to live."
"That's terrible," says the patient, "How can the news possibly be worse?"
The doctor replies, "I've been trying to contact you since yesterday."

Try memorising one, then tell it without missing out any of the story.

The answer to the brainteaser - the surgeon was the boy's mother.

Spool back...
Can you remember one of the tricks you could use for those unexpected moments when someone's name escapes you?

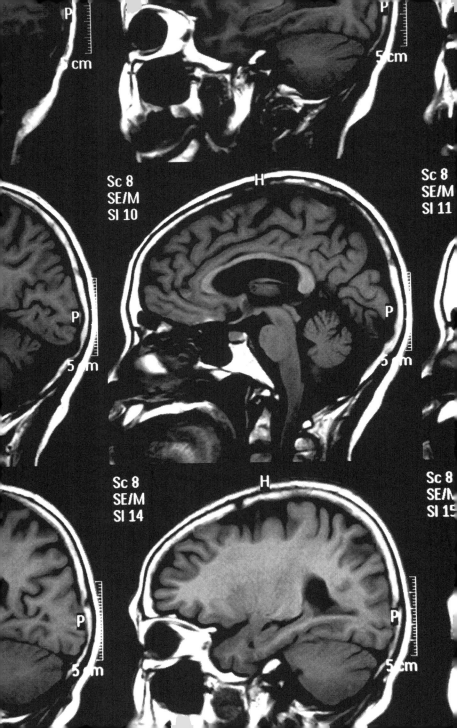

Sc 8
SE/M
SI 10

Sc 8
SE/M
SI 11

Sc 8
SE/M
SI 14

Sc 8
SE/M
SI 15

9. THE FUTURE OF MEMORY

"I intend to make a memory of myself in the minds of others."

– Leonardo de Vinci

Nearly half a century ago when a television series set in the 23rd century arrived on our television screens and Star Trek was launched, we might have noticed a hand-held flip-top communication device being used to make contact between the crew and others on the space craft. In fact, the likeness lead Motorola to name its first flip-phone, 'StarTAC'. Imagining the future has heralded the arrival decades later of many gadgets.

How would it be if it were possible to confirm the accuracy of a memory by checking it against recordings of every event exactly as they took place by means of a tiny, hidden recording device? There would be no more, "But I didn't say that" arguments or, " I would never bring that subject up. You must have started it". The evidence would be jarringly accurate and incontestable.

A TV drama, The Entire History of You, posed just such a dilemma. In it we see a future world in which memories are accessed from a highly sophisticated 'i-World' database. In this world all experiences

- home life, job interviews, holidays, dinner parties, children - are recorded as each character sees them and as they happen by the use of miniature CCTV implants. Tucked behind the ears and wired to the eyes, the camera allows recordings of every moment in each character's life.

These video recordings or objective 'selfies' can then be enjoyed at a later date via an 'action replay' button and can be compared to the recordings of others. Everything is there - holidays, the birth of children, chats with friends, even sexual encounters. Memory, as we used to know and enjoy it becomes conspicuously redundant. Sounds familiar, perhaps? This extension of our Facebook world is perhaps so unsettling because part of the brilliance of memory lies in its uniquely personal quality. A recording is by its nature just that, a record.

Its essence is data input rather than emotional involvement and ultimately it dilutes the overall experience. At present our memories are varied and exclusive. What one person takes from an incident may well be at variance with someone else's but generally we like it that way. And of course, an added advantage is that we can also choose, albeit subconsciously, the relative importance of anything we remember. We can decide on the status of any memory and where we place it in storage for later retrieval. Importantly, we can also change the order of facts to suit our mood or the situation when sharing a story with other people.

Technology, for all its brilliance can become intrusive where memory is concerned and generally unhelpful in human relationships.

For example, when we visit an art gallery, we might look at a painting that features something that touches our emotions and, as a result, jogs our memory. But what happens if we simply take a photo of the picture on the wall - freezing that moment in time only in digital form? Are our emotions and therefore our memory served best by a digital record of an object or the object itself? Being there and later using memory to recall being there may be the key to greater emotional fulfillment. The alternative is to not engage with the present and to serve up a less satisfying digital version of it later on.

In this respect, perhaps dreams are an illustration of the antithesis of recording every event. The world of dreams can be both vivid yet short-lived. Renowned for having a prodigious memory, the painter Salvador Dali had an imagination that allowed him to produce some of the most attention-grabbing art of the twentieth century. His surrealist paintings, supposedly taken from his subconscious and transformed into 'hand painted dream photographs', as he liked to call them, both intrigue and delight us because we recognise the unworldly quality of dreams he captured so well.

When Dali translated his dreams into art, it freed him to explore the far-reaching edges of his own imagination. In his bizarre world of unusual happenings, logical everyday objects are placed in illogical landscapes which stay with us.

In sharp contrast to this, our personal memories of dreams tend to be more transitory and brief. When we first wake up, our thoughts may be full of weird, unfathomable stories from sleep, occasionally so vivid and troubling we feel the need for explanation. But later when we come to recall them, they have vanished. Fragments may remain, but the full story has faded. Here, memory has done its job and wiped the data. (see The Power of Sleep, page 52)

Brain stat: More than 100,000 chemical reactions take place in your brain every second.

Memory's Building Blocks

Is it possible to see the making of a memory action? Theoretically any activity can produce a memory but how exactly does any event turn itself into a memory that can be accessed at a later date? At the Institut de Neurobiologie de la Mediterranee, they think they may have the answer. Scientists there have managed to see the process taking place. The specific neurons used by mice, as they ran on a treadmill or when resting, were identified using a fluorescent protein. The protein, which indicated when the neurons were actively firing, gave the scientists evidence of a memory actually being built when the same neurons were later used by the mice to remember their run.

And, just as for us, the reality of any event can be edited and constructed later as a memory, the same process can, it seems, apply to mice.

During their rest period, the mice produced neuron patterns which were clearly seen to replicate those of the earlier run. The real-time event had now been built into a memory. Not everyone agrees with these findings but it's generally acknowledged that the break through is important and could lead to a clearer understanding of how memory is created.

Mind Probing

MRI scans allow us to see the mind at work as never before and the whole notion of pin-pointing brain function opens up new areas of possibilities. Forget face lifts, we will soon be able to get a quick, cognitive tune up, or as one American brain surgeon put it, 'a brain lift'. What's to stop the healthy mind from being stimulated and given a boost? Brain stimulation techniques are already on the cards to help those who suffer from depression and tuning up our flagging memory might just be what the doctor orders.

Matrix Unleashed

Once a memory is established, the brain can convert it from a short-term version into a long-term one. But what happens if this process fails? Research by scientists into epilepsy has shown that the type of brain activity where long-term memory is lost, can be predicted. They have produced a computer algorithm to match the correct activity and are now in the process of constructing a chip that will activate it. This will eventually will be placed alongside the natural tissue in the brain and trigger normal, or even enhanced long-term memory.

Brain stat: Your brain uses 20% of your body energy but is only 2% of your body weight.

Making It Up

If someone told you they could generate a completely false memory in a person's mind by using a simple recipe of suggestions and prompts, would you believe them?

In her research, Dr. Julia Shaw, a memory scientist and criminal psychologist, did just that by creating a state of 'mis-information' by convincing people that something had taken place (in this case, a crime) when it actually hadn't. The idea of confusing imagination with memory and implanting powerful but false memories proved unexpectedly easy and showed how open to suggestion our recall system can be.

By concocting a precise recipe which involves a 'trusted professional' to mix the ingredients, adding one tub of social pressure, a large cup of falsehood and just enough reality to bind the whole lot together, you have the perfectly fabricated memory cake.

For the brain, attempting to identify which ingredient in the final mix was false then becomes extremely difficult since it will recall the false memory using the same neurons and in the same way as it would a true one.

Astonishingly over 70% of the students taking part in this experiment formed these false memories. The research concluded that the divide between real and false events and the memories they produce are much narrower than we imagined.

Obliterating Memories

If you saw the movie Men in Black, you might remember a gadget dubbed the 'Neuralyzer'. This clever pen-sized device was used by Tommy Lee Jones and Will Smith to obliterate people's recent memories. Now, reality is a step closer to science fiction as scientists are on the point of being able to eradicate a memory and reinstate it again just by taking a pill. Given so much of life's experiences are forgotten and with good reason, should our memories be tampered with and what long-term damage might inadvertently occur if we interfere with our memory bank's hard drive?

In one survey, researchers asked 60 people to take part in an experiment involving pictures of spiders. A proportion of the group were given the beta-blocker drug propranolol and it was with this sub group that the differences in memory became clear. A day later when the beta-blocked individuals were shown the spiders, they exhibited significantly less anxiety than the others who had been drug free. Their memory had been altered to reduce the effect of recalling unpleasant events.

We know that over time the effectiveness of memory will be reduced and a different perspective on an event will take over. But for memory to work successfully it also relies on an underlying capability to recall both good and bad events and this would be compromised by a 'wipe clean' drug. Giving a drug to calm passers-by who had witnessed a fatal car crash would hardly help police with their inquiry and the air accident investigator would be hard pressed to quiz pilots about the failed engine if they couldn't re-member which one had failed. So, balancing the idea of a drug to remove bad memories for those suffering from PTSD (Post Traumatic Stress Disorder) while still allowing a person to remember vital information to 'help police with their enquiries' would be crucial.

Exploring the mechanisms which control and create memory covers new territory and forms the basis of the documentary: Memory Hackers. https:// www.youtube.com/watch?v=mIsIPqYvwUM

Spool back...
Can you remember when the television series Star Trek was set?

"When I first went to school in Czechoslovakia as it then was - nowmodern Slovakia - I must have been about five years old. As I lived in the middle of the countryside where my father was the estate agent, it was considered too far for my young legs to walk the several kilometres to the nearest school. So I was taken by one of the workers on the estate in a horse drawn carriage. I was collected again in the evening, but for lunch I went, as I remember it, all by myself to a nearby family in the village. In those days there was no midday meal served in schools. The people who provided me with the meal did not sit down to eat with me, so I remember hating the isolation of eating alone without my large family around me at table. And I did not enjoy the unfamiliar food either. But I loved the ride in the carriage, and being reunited with my family in the evening."

– Oscar Rakovsky, 101

Index

Made in the USA
Columbia, SC
13 January 2018